COMPARING APPLES TO TACOS

BY RON TETLEY

COMPARING APPLES TO TACOS

HOW TO KNOW WHEN WALL STREET ISN'T PLAYING FAIR WITH YOUR LUNCH MONEY

BY RON TETLEY

DEDICATION

To my wife, Teresa, for putting up with all the late nights and long hours. I could never do or say enough to repay you for the support and help you have been. I love you lots!

To my children, who are all pretty well-grounded and well-behaved (mostly due to their mom). You make me proud.

ACKNOWLEDGEMENTS

I want to thank my business partner, Kip, for the encouragement and support he offered during the process of writing this book. Without him running our business the way he does, I would never have had time to write.

To Callie, our office assistant, who had the unbelievable task of taking my hand-written chicken scratches and typing the rough draft.

To Lisa, my assistant who helped me with all of my service work and made sure I didn't forget about taking care of any clients.

To my wife and my son, Isaac, who helped me proofread and make grammar and writing improvements.

TABLE OF CONTENTS

PREFACE

If you're wondering what tacos and apples have to do with anything, I'll tell you. The expression, "Compare apples to apples," means that if you're going to compare things, make it fair. Don't shine me on. If you're discussing the merits of apples, for instance, don't go comparing them to, say...oranges. Apples and oranges are totally different from each other.

When someone dishonest is trying to pull one over on you, he or she may resort to such discriminatory association tactics to make a buck. The apples-to-tacos thing is my way of expressing what I consider to be the ultimate in such unethical tricks... not only that, but it insults our intelligence. Has this ever happened to you?

Me: "I'd like an apple, please.
Vendor: "Here you go."
Me: "Hey, wait a minute! This is a taco!"
Vendor: "They both taste the same."
Me: "No, they don't!"
Vendor: "Sure they do. That will be $1 please. Enjoy your apple."

Me: "It's a TACO!!"

Vendor: "Whatever."

You can see what I mean about someone trying to convince you of something that all of your senses are telling you is bogus.

As my roots grew deeper and deeper in the financial planning profession, I began to see and hear things I didn't like – things that you would normally associate with hucksters and high-pressure salespeople. I was hearing stories of half-truths, misconceptions and outright lies being passed off by the retail financial planning community as legitimate investment advice. This book is the culmination of years and years of watching this happen, and finally deciding that enough was enough. Someone has to say something.

It is my opinion that the aberrant behavior of a few, if left unchecked, can give any profession a black eye. It is the duty of those of us who believe in honesty and full disclosure to pull back the curtain, so to speak, and expose misinformation and unethical practices one layer at a time. I am a person who likes straight talk and I hope you do, too, because there will be plenty of it in this book. The unpleasant sound you will hear in some of these chapters will be me, raking away the cobwebs of deception to get to the truth, and hacking away at the barnacles of misinformation that have attached themselves to our financial ship.

I love math. I always have. There is a certain truth in math that makes it singularly appealing. Numbers don't lie. Lies are told with words and insinuations that some want to drape over the truth. Truth is usually self-evident, once we remove the layers of confusion put there by those whose purpose truth doesn't serve. It is my hope that as people begin to separate fact from fiction in financial planning, they will share it with friends and family. This will lead to a better understanding of investing as it really is and as it should be, and not as it has been portrayed by retail investment counselors and Wall Street spin doctors. I received much encouragement from colleagues to chronicle these lies and misconceptions who share my disdain for dishonesty. Even so, I would find myself wondering from time to time if this really mattered. What possible difference could one person make? Then I was reminded of the following story:

A man was walking along the shore when he came across thousands of beached starfish. Knowing they would die if they remained on the sand, he began to pick them up and toss them back, one by one, into the safety of the ocean. As he continued this one-at-a-time rescue effort, an onlooker stopped and asked,

"Why are you wasting your time? You will never get to all of them. You will never make a difference."

Without replying, the man bent over, picked up another starfish and tossed it into the water. He turned to the onlooker and said, "I made a difference to that one!"

MAKING A DIFFERENCE

When I was 22, I had just finished with my formal education and had begun my career in corporate America. One day I got a call at work. It was my sister, telling me that I needed to get home right away because our father was killed in a car accident. I was numb. I was speechless. I somehow managed to get home but it felt as if I was on automatic pilot. Nothing seemed real. I was walking down a hallway that kept getting longer and longer.

Another blow came several months later when I learned the details of my mother's financial situation.

Remember the market crash in 1987? Mom and Dad were still recovering from that when the auto accident occurred. With the investment in their 401(k)s, they had lost nearly all their retirement money. I knew my father was working a second job, but I didn't know why until that day, several months after his death. Because of the financial struggles they were having as they tried to make up for the market losses, Dad had to let a big life insurance policy lapse. My mother was left with virtually nothing.

In 1994, when I got into this business, I made a pledge to myself that I was going to protect seniors in retirement the way I was never able to help my parents. I am positive, beyond a shadow of ANY doubt, that if my father had been able to choose some of the safe-money retirement options you will see presented in this book, he would have taken advantage of them. The sad thing is that he was not informed, and my mother struggled as a result of that lack of information.

I am aware of the work cut out for anyone who raises his or her lone voice to expose half-truths and purposeful misconceptions coming from the chorus of many in the retail financial planning community. In my research for this book, I discovered why people in the financial world can get away with some of their propaganda. It's because there is an element within human nature that causes us to *want* to believe grandiose and fanciful promises, even if we know in our gut they can't be true. So I won't be able to help everyone because some will choose to keep the blindfolds on. And I know that some will not agree with my message. They will continue to buy into the same old strategies of the past, regardless of their lack of basis in fact or reason. Some find any change, even a change of mind, difficult. A mind cannot be changed against its will. But I am convinced there will be a few who will appreciate what is revealed here and act on it.

If you're a retiree or approaching retirement, and you picked up this book, you probably know deep down, that there has to be a better strategy for handling your money – one that doesn't require you to risk losing so much of it. You know when you've been told something that just doesn't make sense anymore.

Albert Einstein once said the definition of insanity is to continue doing the same thing over and over again, expecting different results. There comes a time when you have to extend your hand, palm outward, and say, "Hold it! Enough is enough." If you are ready to do this, then I will have done my job and this project was worth the effort.

I heard someone say once, "Those convinced against their will are of the same opinion still." So, I'm not going to give you instructions here ... just information. That way, you'll be able to make an educated decision about what to do with your money.

SECTION I

BROKERS SAY THE
DARNDEST THINGS

I KNOW YOU ARE, BUT WHAT AM I?

One of the most egregious identity assumptions ever pulled off was when German-born Christian Karl Gerhartsreiter moved to the United States as a teenager and began convincing people he was rich and famous. You couldn't really call what he did identity theft because the characters he assumed were completely fictitious. Using the fake name Clark Rockefeller, he established a lavish lifestyle and made a profession out of duping people who really were rich and famous out of their money.

According to journalist Mark Seal, who wrote the book, *The Man in the Rockefeller Suit*, Gerhartsreiter was so brilliant he could have had a legitimate career and earned wealth and fame in his own right. He chose, however, to pull the wool over people's eyes for more than 30 years. His life of deception came to an end in 2008 when his wife of more than 10 years, Sandra Boss, discovered he was a fake and left him, taking their 7-year-old daughter with her. Gerhartsreiter, AKA Clark Rockefeller, was arrested in 2008 after kidnapping the little girl on a court-supervised visit. At this writing, he is still in prison.

While the Gerhartsreiter case makes for interesting reading and our jaws drop at the audaciousness of his lies, his swindling of the upper crust of society seems far away from us on Main Street, USA. But every day, we encounter professionals masquerading as folks they are not. All it takes is a little imagination and the price of a business card, and you can call yourself anything you choose.

Some of the fancy titles people hang on themselves are downright hilarious. One fellow who was a house painter (a perfectly honorable profession, by the way) preferred to refer to himself as a "Color Distribution Technician, LCP." He said the LCP stands for "ladder climbing professional."

Then there was the window washer who gave himself a self-esteem boost with the title, "Transparency-Enhancement Facilitator."

And how about the guy who drove a road sweeper who decided he would introduce himself with a business card on which the fancy script read, "Highway Environmental Hygienist."

Go ahead and chuckle; there is really no harm in that type of misrepresentation. Where I would draw the line, however, would be if someone who didn't attend medical school and wasn't trained or authorized to practice medicine, called himself or herself a doctor, pretending to be qualified to diagnose illnesses and prescribe medicine. Entrusting the outside of your house to a color distribution specialist is one thing. Putting yourself in the care of a doctor wannabe could be downright *dangerous to your health.* Similarly, entrusting your financial planning in retirement to someone who lacks the training and credentials to give you accurate information and proper advice can be *dangerous to your wealth.*

A RETIREMENT PLANNER? REALLY?

All the brokers and financial planners I know of these days are calling themselves *"retirement* planners." They know they aren't, but they say they are. One of my favorite quotes by Abraham Lincoln goes like this: "How many legs does a dog have if you call the tail a leg? Four. Calling a tail a leg doesn't make it a leg."

Just putting a new label on an old jar doesn't change the contents. Nor does adopting the handle of "retirement planner" qualify a stock market broker, or other financial professional, to guide seniors in this unique and precise area of their financial lives.

In most cases, retirees, or those approaching retirement, are cutting the umbilical cord, so to speak, that connects them to what has been their income lifeline – the *paycheck* – and are now moving onto self-support. How retirees and soon-to-be retirees set up their financial affairs at this life junction can make the difference between having a peaceful night's sleep and pacing the floor with worry. Will they have enough money to pay the bills? Will they run out of money after a few years? Will they have to go back to work? Is their nest egg safe from loss? What guarantees do they have?

If a "Retirement Planner" can't answer those questions, he or she should repaint the shingle and toss the business cards into the trash.

Abraham Maslow, the well-known motivational theorist, once said: "If the only tool you have is a hammer, you will see every problem as a nail." Brokers who typically deal only in the stock market where risk is part and parcel of what they do, have only a hammer in their tool box. Any recommendation they make will usually employ some variation of stocks, bonds, and mutual funds. Don't get me wrong. A measure of risk is appropriate for a balanced retirement portfolio, but too much risk can be a lethal poison to that portfolio. If brokers advise older Americans on retirement the same way they would advise a 30-year-old, they could be putting that senior citizen at serious financial risk. This is not play money they are dealing with. To lose a big chunk of your life's savings – money you were counting on to see you through your non-working years of retirement – is a major financial tragedy from which it may be impossible to recover.

Ask seniors who lost as much as 50% of their savings in the 2008 stock market plunge if risk matters. Ask those retirees who saw the Wall Street ticker wipe out a substantial portion of their nest egg in a single day if they trust an investing formula that includes too much risk.

BABY BOOMERS!

Why do so many financial people want to jump on the retirement planning bandwagon? Two words – baby boomers.

Baby boomers are those Americans born between 1947 and 1964. When American soldiers came home from fighting overseas in World War II, they did what you would have expected them to do. They settled down, found jobs, and raised families. Naturally, a dramatic surge in the birthrate ensued (thus the term, *baby boom*). The Depression of the 1930s was over and American factories were producing again, and so were American moms. As the members of this generation passed through each stage of their lives, they changed the shape of the country's economic and social landscape and set the economic pace for American life. Boomers were the buyers and sellers of cars, homes, televisions, radios, computers, and appliances.

Boomers had such an appetite for whatever the country's horn of plenty could produce that they invented a new device they called the "credit card," which they would proceed to use more and more as the years went by. The cornucopia kept producing and the Boomers kept buying. Installment credit was once an arrangement between a big department store, like Macy's or JCPenney, and the individual customer. With the advent of the credit card, however, revolving charge accounts became a national phenomenon. Boomers could just say "charge it," take it home, and pay for it later.

Socially and scientifically, the boom generation transformed the face of America. Their forefathers may have invented airplanes, but it was the Boom generation that dreamed and carried out the seemingly impossible – putting a human footprint on the surface of the moon. Boomers invented rock-and-roll music. They were children of the nuclear age and learned to live with the unspoken terror of what came to be called "the bomb." More than any generation that had come before, they were movers and shakers, dreamers and doers.

And now, they are ready to retire. If you go by the U.S. Census Bureau statistics, the very first Baby Boomer turned 65 on January 1, 2011. The first batch of the 78 million boomers alive today is rushing headlong toward retirement like spawning salmon. Some in this retirement stampede have their acts together; they planned ahead. They know exactly how much they need each month to live on after their paychecks from work stop coming in. They saved adequately and have the pieces of the puzzle all lined up and ready to snap neatly together. Unfortunately, according to most surveys, these prudent planners are in the minority, outnumbered by those who overspent and failed to plan.

Boomers as a class have never been all that good at saving for retirement and, still feeling the impact of the Great Recession of 2008, they are even less prepared for it now. The Transamerica Center for Retirement Studies found that 54% of workers age 60 and above have not saved enough for retirement. The Employee Benefit Research Institute reported that only 14% felt confident they would be able to live comfortably in retirement.

So it is no wonder, then, that we see so many in the financial trades adopting the handle, "Retirement Planner." Sensing there is money to be made, they are showing up like umbrella vendors in a rainstorm.

There is no denying Baby Boomers need some help in the area of retirement planning. Social Security, even if it is able to continue to keep its promises, is proving to be merely a helpful side fund for this new pack of retirees, not the mainstay it was for their parents' generation. What about pensions? Some Boomers have them and some don't. Those who do should consider themselves fortunate. Pensions are disappearing from the American workplace the way buffalo vanished from the Great Plains. Defined *benefit* plans began phasing out as defined *contribution* plans, such as the 401(k) took over in the 1990s.

Pensions guaranteed a lifetime income, but the proceeds from 401(k)'s flow only until the well runs dry and are typically based on stock market gains and losses. Since these accounts are primarily invested in mutual funds, the sudden market free falls of 2000 and 2008 caused no small degree of worry. Volatility and flat returns following the 2008 market crash put a big question mark on the viability of 401(k) plans as reliable income sources in retirement. Although the investing public may be jaded about 401(k) investments, for the most part they don't know where else to turn.

TO EVERYTHING THERE IS A SEASON

Many people from the generation that gave us rock and roll are having a hard time sensing their limitations. Their panache for breaking tradition and pushing the envelope is reflected in their vision of retirement. Unlike their parents, whose idea of retirement involved idle days and rocking chairs, this new bunch expects their "sunset years" to be characterized by gym memberships, Mediterranean cruises, dance lessons, and sports cars. More and more seniors seek financial answers that aren't forthcoming from the mainstream investment mills. Having experienced disappointment in the stock market performance, they're looking for the word "guarantee" in their financial planning. But they're finding many of the so-called retirement planners don't seem to have that word in their vocabularies.

Fact: The closer you are to retirement, the more conservative you need to be with your assets. Let's face it...when it comes to saving and managing money, what makes sense for someone in their 20s and 30s doesn't make sense for someone who is ready to retire.

To illustrate – If you are in your 60s, would you approach your life physically the same way you did in your 20s? Likely not. Sixty may be the new 40, but it would be utter foolishness for seniors to treat their bodies with the recklessness of a teenager. On the contrary, caring for your physical resources is one way to make sure you keep them as long as possible.

It is the same with financial resources. You don't play fast and loose with your assets as you approach retirement. Yankee baseball great Mickey Mantle is credited with saying, "If I knew I was going to live this long, I would have taken better care of myself." I don't know who said, "Save your money; you may need it someday," but I certainly agree with the sentiment. Brokers turned retirement counselors are just wrong, wrong, wrong to suggest raw market investments as safe havens for retirement portfolios. As a financial professional who specializes in helping those entering retirement do so comfortably and with as much security as possible, I have to conclude this misguided advice comes from either an intentional desire to mislead, or from the good intentions of one who is ill-equipped and poorly educated in the ways of safe investment strategies. Because I wish to keep my faith in human nature intact, I want to believe the latter, but it's probably a combination of both.

CHAPTER TWO

IT'S MY BALL AND WE'LL PLAY BY MY RULES!

We move through life in phases, and there are two distinct phases to our financial lives, as well. The first is called the *Accumulation Phase*. This is when we work hard and earn a living for our families. We are accumulating not only houses, cars, and furniture, but hopefully, a nest egg of savings for the day when we will stop working and enter the *Distribution Phase*. This is when we use our accumulated wealth to fund retirement. Combined with Social Security payments, pension payments, and any financial arrangements we made, we use what portion of our savings necessary to meet expenses. When we die, we hope to pass the remainder of these funds on to our loved ones.

Baby Boomers may have had productive working relationships with brokerage houses and their agents during their accumulation years. Their accounts may have flourished during their working days when they were able to feed their investment accounts with regular deposits. That is well and good and proper. Dollar cost averaging during one's working years is one of the best methods for achieving capital growth.

DOLLAR COST AVERAGING

Dollar cost averaging works when you make steady, regular contributions to an investment fund, and continue to make them over time, creating a win/win situation for yourself. No matter what the stock market does, you make money. During one's accumulation years, this is a prudent use of resources. When workers contribute, say $100 per month, into a 401(k) plan, which in turn invests that money in mutual funds, every time that money is deposited, shares are bought at whatever the market price is at the time. If the market is on the rise, and share prices are soaring, no problem; your account grows along with the surge. But what about when the market sags, and share prices drop? Still, there is no problem, as long as you make those same regular deposits into the investment account. Why? Because when share prices dropped, your dollar went further. Your $100 bought more shares. Those skinny shares will eventually fatten and your account prospers accordingly. Given the behavior of the stock market, you should always come out ahead, as long as you keep up your contributions.

What happens when you move from the *accumulation phase* to the *distribution phase* of life? You must now switch gears. It's time to preserve what you have and enter a different mode of behavior and thinking when it comes to money. Otherwise, you will get caught in the *reverse dollar cost averaging* trap. What's that? It means just what it says, and it can be as bad for you in your later years as dollar cost averaging was good for you in your younger years.

Think about it. You're retired. You are in full-blown distribution mode. Your paychecks no longer roll in and your regular contributions to your investment account have stopped. Hopefully, you consulted a retirement specialist and moved that money out of harm's way and into an investment vehicle specifically designed to house retirement accounts for the distribution phase. But if you leave your money parked in the same spot where you kept it during the accumulation years, and begin paying yourself a salary out of your nest egg, you are *withdrawing* money from that account with the same regularity as you *deposited* money into it – with one major difference. The amount you withdraw is greater. When it comes time for your regular monthly check to be cut from the brokerage house to your checking account, or sent to your mailbox, *you sell shares* of those stocks or mutual funds to produce that income. What if the market is on a roll? You sell fewer shares to produce the income because each share you sell is worth more. But what if the market is going down? You are forced to sell shares anyway, and now you must sell more of them to produce the income you need. Factor in also that you deplete the account faster. Every share you sell is that many fewer shares you have working for you. Many seniors who felt the sting of reverse dollar cost averaging in the stock market crash of 2008 began to understand that their brokers weren't necessarily telling them the whole story with their long-term projections. The sad part is, once those shares are gone, there is no replacing them.

SHIFTING GEARS

Ultimately, recognizing when it is time to shift gears is the investor's responsibility. Financial professionals are ethically bound to inform clients of their options when this transition in their financial lives approaches. Sadly, some who have had a productive working relationship with clients for a long time during the working years don't inform them when it is not in their best interests to have the bulk of their resources at risk in the market. What is even more reprehensible is when they begin to think of these clients as a captive audience and convince them they should continue to rely on them for advice and guidance during distribution phase, knowing they are no longer in a position to guide them.

"Safety? You want safety? Hey, we got safety... it's called money market!"

What's wrong with that picture? Have you checked the return on money market funds lately? At this writing, money markets are returning less than one percent. What's inflation at right now? Three percent? What about CDs? They're safe, right? Yes, but their returns aren't much better.

I am going out on a limb here to say that when a person reaches adulthood, they should no longer seek medical treatment from a pediatrician. It's not that their pediatricians weren't good doctors. They were probably fine physicians in their area of expertise. But you have changed. Your body isn't the same as it was when you were a child.

Likewise, when people in their 60s approach retirement, they don't need the same advice as people who are in their 20s, new to the work force, and just starting a family. Nor do they identify with those in their 30s and 40s, who are still working and saving, with years to go before retirement. No one will debate that point on its face. But many, it seems, won't question the credentials or the motives of brokers suddenly turned retirement planners.

BASEBALL RULES IN A FOOTBALL GAME

Most of our adult life is spent in the accumulation phase —from our late teens/early 20s until perhaps our late 50s/early 60s. We may spend 40 to 50 years in this phase.

At first, this phase seems awkward. We don't understand the rules, and we are not really comfortable. But as time goes on, we begin to understand our jobs and we become better at managing our money. To use a baseball analogy, think of how you would feel if you suddenly found yourself in a baseball stadium for the first time, and you were expected to play the game. You are awkward and uncomfortable. You don't understand the rules, and you're more than a little confused. What are those bags? What do these lines mean? What is that mound in the middle of the field? You don't know how to hit the ball; you don't know how to catch it. You don't know how to play the game. Heck, you can't even find center field!

But after some practice you start to get the hang of it. The longer you're in that stadium, the more you learn the game. You learn the rules, the players, the teams, all of it. After a while you even get good at looking at the stats and analyzing teams and players at their various skill levels. You become so comfortable with the game that playing baseball becomes second nature to you. If the coach says, "We are out in the field," you know exactly what is happening and where you fit in. If the coach says, "We are up to bat," you know everybody's role and responsibility.

But one day, the owner of the team comes in with bundles of new uniforms and strange headgear called helmets, and tells everybody that he is changing over from baseball to football. The field is completely redone to resemble a gridiron with yard markers and goal posts. You've never played football. The coach has never coached football, but he insists that there can't be that much difference.

That's what it is like when you switch from the accumulation phase and go into the distribution phase with a financial coach who is still trying to play by the accumulation phase rules. It just doesn't work.

Can you imagine standing in the middle of the football field, looking for the bases? There are none! The distribution phase has a completely different set of rules by which to play. And here is your old baseball coach telling you, "Don't worry. I have the old baseball rulebook and we can play by those rules just as well."

Here's your taco.

Go ahead and try, but if you're playing football with baseball rules, you'll never win.

In the distribution phase of our financial lives, the tax rules are different, objectives are completely different, and your perspective on safety, growth, and liquidity are dramatically different. If you try to run the distribution phase of your life the same way you ran the accumulation phase, you will hurt yourself financially and wind up frustrated and confused.

Switch gears. Learn the new rules of the game. Get a coach who knows what he or she is doing.

A competent distribution coach will understand this new game and how to play by its rules. If your broker says he/she does retirement planning, but all you see are the same old plays, this is what detectives and people in criminal forensics would call a "*clue*" that perhaps it's time to get a new coach.

The ball game has changed, and it's not that your old broker did a poor job; it's just time to move on.

CHAPTER THREE

STOP HITTING YOURSELF.
STOP HITTING YOURSELF.
STOP HITTING YOURSELF.

When I was a young parent and my four children were little fireballs, full of energy, I used to love playing with them until we were so tired none of us could move. It wasn't wrestling, really, although there was some of that. It was a combination of romping, tickling, and tumbling.

One of our favorite games involved me being a human spring board. I would lie on my back with my knees bent and my feet firmly planted flat on the ground. They would line up, one in front of the other, all four of them, each one about 20 feet apart, and run toward me as fast as they could. With their arms outstretched, they would plant their hands on my knees, tuck their heads, and I would catch them by their shoulders as they continued the roll, catapulting them into a complete forward flip. They would hopefully land several feet past my head and go get back in line for another run. The injuries were never really that bad, but looking back I ask myself, "Why did I do it?" My dad did it with my brother and me. I never thought twice about playing hard and being physical with my children.

Another one of my favorite games was to take my kids' hands at the wrist and playfully make them slap themselves in the face. As I was making them slap themselves, I would say over and over, "Stop hitting yourself! Stop hitting yourself! Stop hitting yourself!"

It was such great fun.

I meet with people every day who have been going through what amounts to the same thing, only with real harm as a result. It is as if their arms are being held by someone they know and trust and who has control over their finances, and who is making them do unpleasant and hurtful things with their money. Their brokers have a firm grip on them, so to speak, making them slap their own faces over and over financially only it's no game. Losing big chunks of your life savings is serious business. It is as if these hapless clients are the objects of some cruel practical joke that never ends.

I can't tell you how many times (too many to count) that I've had couples come into my office complaining about something their broker did or did not do. One couple stands out in my memory because they were so angry. They felt their broker wrecked their lives, putting them in a precarious position. They had lost a significant portion of their portfolio just as they were counting down to retirement. Now they were forced to change their plans.

"I had to go back to my old boss and plead to continue working," said the husband. "I figure I will be there at least another three years ... if I can get my old job back."

"We told our broker what we wanted, and it was as if he wasn't even listening to us. He talked us into doing something we really didn't understand," the wife said.

The couple said that, in the end, they were intimidated by the inference the broker made that, with his experience and knowledge of the movements of the stock market, he knew what was best and they should just "trust the expert."

"I just assumed he knew things that we didn't, and it was best to shut up and let him do his job," said the woman, ruefully.

Brokers sometimes use the magic pixie dust of one-liners and worn out clichés designed to eliminate doubt and convince the client all will be well if they just do as they're told. These magic sayings seem to mesmerize the client, like the pendulum a hypnotist uses. The brokers proceed onward, slapping the clients' faces with their own hands while the decisions the brokers make about where and how to position their money is playing havoc with the clients' retirement.

MAGIC SAYINGS

"You're in it for the long haul." Did we tell you our ages? You did understand that we're senior citizens, right? We are in our sunset years. How long of a haul is required in order for the market to recover from that last nosedive? I'm glad we're in it for the long haul. I would hate to see what would happen if we were in it for the short haul.

"Buy low, sell high." This is a great one! I don't think anyone could have figured that out on their own. This advice means you know when the next downturn will occur, right? Because that's when you are going to use my money to buy, right? Well, if you have that kind of ability, then you can call me the day before a stock market crash and alert me that it is time to pull the plug on all the market positions and move to the safety of cash, right? And you have my phone number, right?

"Dollar cost average" You did understand we're approaching retirement? Dollar cost averaging is great when you're young, but it works in the reverse when you retire. Did they teach you that in broker school?

"Don't worry, it will come back." - What you mean is, leave my assets invested in the market positions that have just cost me half my life savings because, eventually, they will recover and I'll be back to even, right? What if it takes a long time to come back? What if I need some of my money in three years and it takes 10 years to come back?

Also, let me see if I have the "come back" math straight. You're saying that if the market loses 50% and then recovers 50% then I am back to even, right? WRONG! Math was always easy for me, so let me illustrate it simply. If a person's assets drop 50%, it takes more than a 50% recovery for them to get back to where they started.

To break even, the market would not only have to go back to where it was before the crash... but because I had less money working for me, it would have to go up, not the 50% that it lost, but 100%!

If you invested $100,000 and lost 50%, you'd have $50,000 remaining. Now if you earn 50% on your $50,000 balance, that is only $25,000, bringing your new account value to $75,000. You would have to earn 100% on the $50,000 balance to get back to your original value. This is why most people in retirement will never see their accounts get back to break-even in their lifetime after a big loss occurs.

There are more magic pixie dust sayings brokers use to justify playing fast and loose with the

Losses and Recovery

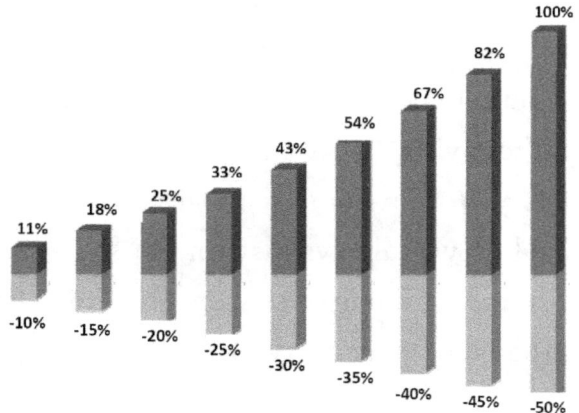

assets of retirees and people approaching retirement,

and I'll cover some of those later in this book. The problem with these sayings is they sound like they should be true when you first hear them.

Take, "Just hang in there and it will come back," for example. That statement is only true in a situation where you don't need the money and won't need it for some time. Remember, what worked in the past will not work when you are in the distribution phase. It's a different ball game

Back when you didn't need the money and you had 15-plus years before you would need it, those sayings may have made sense for you. But the pixie dust doesn't work in the retirement phase of life, folks. Just because someone who earned your trust in the past is now holding your wrists and making you slap yourself, doesn't make the advice they are giving you any truer. If that is your situation, then get out now. Stop hitting yourself!

Ron Tetley

CHAPTER FOUR

EENIE, MEENIE, MINEY, MO

Everyone loves a good magic trick.

When American magician David Copperfield performed his trick "Walking through the Great Wall of China" on television in 1986, the world watched in awe. Filmed before a live audience on both sides of the wall, the slender magician entered the Great Wall from one side, and emerged moments later on the other side. The trick catapulted Copperfield to worldwide fame and the television special earned two Emmy Award nominations.

Now, tell the truth. Do you really believe that a man actually walked through a 20-foot thick stone wall? Of course not. But we are suckers for illusion. We want to believe.

The Hermann Grid, named after German psychologist and speech scientist Ludimar Hermann, is a classic example of optical illusion. It is a grid of black boxes separated by thick, white lines. At every intersection of these white lines, our eyes perceive a grey dot. But when we try to look directly at these dots, they disappear. Just let your eyes relax, however, and other dots appear.

Yep, we have a tendency to believe the unbelievable sometimes. Approximately one-third of the brain is dedicated to vision while only 8% is dedicated to touch and 3% to hearing. Seeing what is not there is a result of trying to reconcile the mixed signals our brains sometimes get from our senses.

The Penrose Triangle, first created by Swedish artist Oscar Reutersvärd in 1934, is another good one. Every time you look at it, the lines fold back on themselves. You know that's impossible, but that is what your brain is telling you. The triangle leans toward you in one glance and away from you in another. Roger Penrose, an English mathematician and philosopher, popularized the object when he used it in his lectures to illustrate how reality is often far different from what we perceive.

What does all that have to do with the financial world? Several myths or illusions in the retail financial world have been created so that you, as an investor/consumer, would believe the retail story. This fictional story has many twists and turns and, like any good sci-fi thriller, it sounds truthful because of the half-truths and misconceptions it contains. It is important to those in the retail financial world that you buy into these concepts because these folks only make money when you give them your money. And, oh, yes...don't *ever* ask questions as to what they plan to do with your money, or you'll risk being labeled a troublemaker. Just hand it over to them and they'll generate activity that they can charge you for on the next account statement. Never mind that they get paid regardless of whether or not you are benefited by that activity.

Let us take a look at the three biggest illusions being pitched in the retail world of financial planning today.

1. "Give me your money and I can pick the stocks that will yield the best return for you on your investment." Deep down inside, I think we all know that this is simply not possible. *Yet the illusion excites us.* We want to believe we found the amazing

Crisco...the wizard who was somehow imbued with the ability to predict the stock market.

Think about it this way: If someone truly did know how to pick stocks, wouldn't they have already done it for themselves? They would be the Houdini of the financial planning world. Why, everyone from Wall Street, Washington, and all the networks would be beating a path to their door. Any reasoning, thinking person knows that this is an impossibility, but for some reason the retail market still tries to sell us the illusion that they can do it. They also claim to have the magical ability to study a company's stock and tell you whether that company will thrive or fail ... whether the company's profits will rise or fall.

Truth alert: Most of the time, even the CEOs of the companies don't know what their profits will be in the next three to six months (much less one to two years). If the CEOs don't know, how does anyone outside the company have a chance at knowing?

The retail world will tell you they have ways of knowing when the stock of a certain company is overvalued or undervalued. Stock market prices are determined by a litany of factors, from company earnings and the economy, to world news, fear and greed, oil prices, world events, natural disasters, and a host of others. With more than 7 billion people on this earth, not even Nostradamus could possibly predict what the actions of any of those billions of people will be, or foretell how those actions will impact any one company's product or service at any given time. It's impossible! That information is unknowable and unpredictable.

The actions of the entire world are already factored into the price of a stock. Since the *only* information that can possibly change the price of the stock going forward is unknowable and unpredictable, and since no person possesses this, we shake our heads in disbelief when we hear certain advisers still weaving the illusion that they can predict stock prices, or know someone who can know it.

Truth alert: No matter how many pie charts, graphs, reports, and computer programs you bring into the equation, you and I simply cannot predict the future ... only the past. If these market gurus really could pick stocks, then none of their clients would lose a dime.

Serving as sort of a *Consumer Reports* for the investment world, Dalbar, Inc., an independent research firm based out of Boston, Mass., conducts an annual study called the "Quantitative Analysis of Investor Behavior" (QAIB). The QAIB documents and reviews the long-term results of tens of thousands of actual investor returns. In 2011, the QAIB study revealed that the average investor underperformed in the stock market by nearly 8%.

Since the QAIB's inception more than 20 years ago, Dalbar, Inc.'s overall long-term findings have shown that investment advisors return only about half of what the market is able to generate on its own.

All I'm saying is that if the stock market wizards with their magic charts and graphs are truly able to predict the market, then they should be able to beat it, right?

2. "I know when it is the best time to get in and out of the stock market." It's called "timing the market" and it doesn't work. I will say it again. If anyone really knew how to do this, they would own all the money in the world.

In fact, they would eventually kill the market. No one would buy and sell. What would be the point?

In a nutshell, here's why "timing the market" doesn't work:

There are 5,040 trading days on Wall Street in a 20-year period. Look at what a difference it makes to miss the target on just a few of those days.

Let's use Dalbar's research on the 20 years between January 1, 1989, and December 31, 2008. If you had put $10,000 money in an index fund, one that simply mirrored the market each day, and left it there, never trying to "time" the market by getting in or out at certain times or picking stocks, you would average a return of 8.43% per year. That is the pure market return for those 20 years, during which your $10,000 investment would have turned into $50,455.

Why Market Timing Doesn't Work

January 1, 1989 - December 31, 2008

5,040 Trading Days	Return of S&P 500 Index	Growth of $10,000 Investment
Stay Fully Invested	8.43%	$50,455
Missed the 5 Best Days	6.27%	$33,720
Missed the 10 Best Days	4.89%	$26,006
Missed the 15 Best Days	3.65%	$20,500
Missed the 20 Best Days	2.58%	$16,630
Missed the 25 Best Days	1.57%	$13,654
Missed the 30 best Days	.61%	$11,283

But what if you missed the best five days of the market? Your gain would have been only 6.27% and your $10,000 would have only grown to $33,720. Or if you missed 10 days, your gain would be 4.89% and so forth.

What's the point? If you're trying to time the market, then you had better be perfect or it will cost you. The truth is, you can't time the market. It's never been done successfully. People who claim they were successful were either lucky a time or two, or they are lying.

3. "I can't predict the stocks or time the market, but we have some really smart guys at the home office who can."

You would like to commend them for admitting an inability here, but then that last part just sort of stops you cold, doesn't it? They *don't* have any really smart guys at the home office who can predict stocks or time the market. They may get it right a few times quite by accident, more or less the same way you could call heads or tails correctly five or six times in a row and make the crowd watching you think you were blessed with mental telepathy.

Ever heard of "hindsight bias"? Here's how it works: Let's say you have 1,100 people standing in a room and you give each of them a quarter. Now you tell everyone to flip the quarter, and if they get heads they get to remain standing. If they get tails, they have to sit down. So they all flip the quarter and about half of them sit down. You tell the half left standing to flip the quarter again. Heads stay standing and tails sit down. Again, around half will sit down because that is the odds of a coin toss. Kids know that.

If you do this 10 times, out of eleven hundred people you had in the beginning, you will have about 6-12 people still standing at the end. Imagine the luck! Flipping a coin and getting heads 10 times in a row! Does this mean the people left standing studied the quarter for its thickness and weight, and analyzed the metal for its aerodynamic characteristics so as to determine which way it would land? Did they do an in-depth study on the relation of the kinetic energy released by the flip itself, and calculate how high the coin should elevate, how many revolutions it should make as it spun in mid-air, and at what precise moment the quarter should land showing heads up? No. They just got lucky.

Now take a mutual fund company with 1,100 funds in its family of funds. The representative shows you how a handful of their fund managers beat the market the last 10 years in a row. Does this mean they know how to study stocks or when to get in and out of the market? No. They flipped heads. But you have to hand it to the mutual fund company, don't you? It is a nice illusion. It's a nice parlor trick to parade those lucky guys around and let them pretend they know something that everyone else seems not to know. It makes the vulnerable and trusting souls line up to put their money on the counter, so to speak.

But like all good magic tricks, they allow you to see only what they want you to see and conceal the rest. Where are the mutual fund family dogs? Why weren't they part of the parade? Where's the information you didn't want me to see? That's like a magician coming on stage and telling you that earlier, there was an elephant on stage, but I made it disappear just before you came in for the show.

Truth alert: If mutual fund managers really knew how to pick stocks or time the market, how many funds would the mutual fund company need? One. And in that fund, how many investments would they ever need to hold at one time? One.

WE WANT TO BELIEVE

The problem with us is that we want to believe. We want to think there is some computer program that works with algorithms and can predict which way the market will go. We want to park our money with a guru and sit back and let that guru make us wealthy by picking stocks. We want to believe that someone has the magic touch with the buy/sell button and can maneuver through the minefield of the stock market, buying low and selling high. That's one of the reasons why the illusions they throw at us work so well – we want to believe. It's like that Penrose Triangle. We know it's an illusion, but we're still drawn to it.

Remember David Copperfield. He specialized in making things disappear. Perhaps the most famous object he made vanish was the Statue of Liberty. Don't fall for fancy illusions designed to make your money disappear as well.

SECTION II

WILL SOMEONE PLEASE TURN THE TV DOWN!!

CHAPTER ONE

MEDIA NOISE

It is believed humans first began to communicate long distance by striking a hollow log with a tree limb. The sound could travel miles if the log was dry and the limb was sturdy and the wind was just right. The distant recipient of the crude message would then send back a rhythmic answering signal from another hollow log. Then someone discovered that by stretching an animal skin tightly across one of the open ends and striking the leather membrane, the sound would carry twice as far. A network of these jungle drums could allow villages to communicate with each other over hundreds of miles. The information age had begun.

How far we have come! Today we are awash with communication. Thirty years ago if you were to tell someone that you were "tweeting" on your

"Twitter account," that you were "behind on your email" because you spent too much time posting on your Facebook page the night before, you'd get a blank stare and one of those are-you-losing-it looks. Wonder what they would think of your smart phone?

We are experiencing an information Tsunami these days. There is such a free flow of information that our fund of knowledge is only limited by our curiosity. How could this wealth of information possibly be a bad thing, you ask? If information were water, it would be the same as trying to quench our thirst for it by drinking from the nozzle of a fire hose. It has just become too much.

Have you noticed the increasing flow of financial information these days? It's everywhere you look. There must be at least a dozen channels devoted to money and finance on my local cable service. And those are just the ones I'm aware of. Nationwide, hundreds of programs broadcast at all hours of the day and night, each spewing opinions from talking heads shown in front of scrolling data to back up their points of view. With this kaleidoscope of noise and numbers, is it any wonder information has turned to confusion?

Back in the 1970s, one of the most popular segments of the CBS news program *60 Minutes* was a three-minute debate entitled *Point/Counterpoint,* where two opposing political viewpoints were aired. The original feature allowed two commentators to bicker in front of the cameras. It was good television, but it was replaced by Andy Rooney's segment, which ended the show on a light-hearted and often poignant note about American life in general. Then, during the late 1990s, the point-counterpoint format was resurrected in a big way by the cable channels devoted to the stock market and all things financial. If you listen to these talking heads, it will make yours spin in confusion.

"Invest in energy; it's going through the roof!"

"Stay away from energy! It's only a matter of time before the bottom will drop out."

"Tighten your belts! We're in for three more years of recession."

"Recession? What recession? Happy days are here again!"

Then there's the fellow who comes on wearing a clown suit, blowing a kazoo and ringing a cowbell. He talks about which stocks to buy and which ones to leave alone. How are we supposed to regard this part of the program? It appears to be comedy, but he's serious about his recommendations and seems genuinely angry when he is in attack mode. It makes you wonder what's next. Stock picking by a talking mule?

If you want a real experience in the agreement/ disagreement of conflicting investing theory, just visit the magazine section of your local bookstore. I did. There were a few magazines I'd heard about before, some of which have been around for decades, and then there are new magazines on the rack with names I found completely unfamiliar. All of them seemed to shout at me, competing for attention with headlines that resemble those of the cheap tabloid newspapers and other landfill fodder.

"Penny Stocks That Will Be Worth
a Fortune!"
"Twenty-Five Ways to Earn 200%
Over Five Years"
"Triple Your Money – What's LUCK
Got to Do With It?"

Oh boy. Pass the antacid tablets.

THE INTERNET

The internet is a never-ending cornucopia of data and information. Just boot up your favorite browser and type the word "stocks" into the search bar. You will literally get hundreds of millions of search results. The information bombardment is overwhelming and nearly all of it is conflicting. Is it any wonder a seeker of truth and reason will have a difficult time recognizing it when he or she finds it?

There is something out there these days that I call "financial pornography." This is where slick con artists in silk suits pose as gurus imbued with special knowledge about investing. They clear their throats and speak in arrogant tones about investing as if to disagree with them would be the highest form of heresy. To those who are knowledgeable, their bias is shocking. And yet they spread it as if it were gospel over the airwaves and in the print media to a gullible public, when all the while, their motives are to line their own pockets. To me, they take advantage of the public's desire to have someone lead them out of the confusion of conflicting investing theories and into the light of a safe place where they can earn a reasonable rate of return without losing their life savings. But instead, they find themselves drawn in like cult children down a road of too much risk and too little reward.

Whenever you wonder why a magazine or the internet, for example, comes out with an article throwing rocks at a particular investing strategy, you'll find your answer at the end of the money trail. Follow the money trail and you'll see full-page advertisements by those who make money if you believe their cleverly concealed spiels.

Brokers and financial firms who want you to believe they have the magic beans will come out with an article proclaiming some angle of investing that sounds plausible enough when you see it. Or they may condemn another strategy that doesn't have their stamp of approval, mainly because they don't make any money if you go in that direction. They pay for advertising and the media sources print whatever they say. The media loves it when people predict the future. That sells magazines. Whether the prediction tells of good times to come or bad times around the corner really doesn't matter. In case you didn't know it, stock brokers collect their fees regardless of the outcome of your trading account. Just offer a prediction and you'll get a voice, either in the print columns or on the money talk shows. Predictions are great press. Don't worry if you are dead wrong. You won't get called on the carpet. Your reputation won't be ruined. Everybody makes mistakes. You'll probably be invited back to explain what little detail you missed that threw you off track.

"But wait a minute, Ron," I can hear you saying. "Some of these people's predictions come true!"

Yes, well, even a broken clock is right two times a day. Does that mean it's an accurate timepiece? Not on my planet.

Let me share with you what some of the most prestigious universities and colleges teach fledgling investment advisors to do to begin their illustrious careers as prognosticators and soothsayers. First, they tell them, go out and buy a mailing list of 10,000 people who have asset-producing investments. There are a bazillion places from which to buy these and they cost pennies per record. The next step, they say, is to go to work showing the people on the list how good they are at picking investments. The mailer will typically include a simple, one-page letter. One letter, sent to 5,000 people on the list, will offer the prediction that company A's stock will go up in value. The other letter will tell the other 5,000 recipients that company A's stock will go down in value. At the end of the week, if company A's stock went up, you keep that list of 5,000 and throw away the other 5,000 names.

Now a new letter goes out telling 2,500 on the good list that company B's stock will go up next week.

The other 2,500 get a letter saying the opposite. At the end of the next week, you keep one list and throw the other one away. You get the idea. If you're correct in your predictions twice in a row to 2,500 people, wow! You must really know what you're doing.

But wait... it gets better. Now you mail a letter to 1,250 people predicting that company C's stock will go up next week. The other 1,250 are told that company C's stock will go down. At the end of that week, you now have 1,250 people who think you are a genius because you have been right three times in a row.

Think about it. If you do this for five weeks, you will end up with 312 people who received letters from you in which your predictions were right on the money. How many of those 312 people will give you all their money, asking you to manage it for them and work your magic? Those who don't line up at your office door will receive a phone call and you can play the role of The Great Kreskin, seer of seers and prognosticator of prognosticators. Good for business? Absolutely! Ethical? Well, perhaps you broke no laws, but you gave new meaning to the Latin phrase, *Caveat Emptor* – Let the buyer beware!

It goes without saying that these advisors know nothing out of the ordinary. They're guessing, the same as your eight-year-old daughter could. In fact, you could probably out-perform 80% of the brokers on Wall Street by throwing a handful of papers in the air, each paper bearing a stock symbol on one side, and buying the ones that land face up.

I am constantly amazed at how the media loves to promote anyone who has the chutzpah (Yiddish for "audacity") to make a prediction, no matter how outlandish it is. The very fact that a prediction is made creates an air of mystery. A breathless public waits to see if it will come true or not. It's good television. It moves the merchandise.

Listen closely to some of the introductions of these television prognosticators and you'll notice they have thin credentials, if any at all. But that doesn't seem to matter much.

What drops out of the bottom for the poor consumer is a static-filled harsh sound and an endless stream of conflicting information. In fact, there is so much information and noise that it seems impossible to sort through and make sense of it all. For the average investor, the confusion leaves them paralyzed. They can't all be right, so the decision to freeze like a deer in the headlights seems to be the right one to make...a move that can have disastrous consequences for someone planning his or her retirement.

The point is these showmen who rule the media are not above lining their pockets at your expense. Erroneous information disseminated by the weather person on the 11 o'clock news may ruin your weekend plans. But erroneous information put out by these folks can ruin your life.

CHAPTER TWO

INVESTMENT LIES

I hate being lied to. I feel utter resentment when I discover that something I've been told isn't true. I remember feeling this way even as a child. I know my parents didn't mean anything by it...they were just following tradition... but I felt the most profound sense of betrayal when I discovered there was no such thing as (warning! warning! Spoiler alert for readers under the age of seven!) a corpulent, bearded, elf from the North Pole who wore a size triple-X red suit and, with the assistance of flying reindeer, circled the globe as the world's most famous toy philanthropist.

I understood the lie about Santa Claus wasn't a malicious one. But it still hurt. And it made me sad to discover how many layers of deception had been employed over all those years to make the lie believable. And to think that it was all the clever handiwork of the two people in the world I loved and trusted the most (just kidding, mom). When our first daughter, Shawnie, came along, however, I found myself weaving the same story for her. When she lost her first tooth, I even spun out the one about a fairy who placed great value on lost incisors and bicuspids and might just visit her pillow that night.

I suppose those fairy tales were harmless enough. But when people who claim to be professionals lie to you about money...*your* money... that becomes another matter entirely. You don't expect an accountant, for example, to lie to you about your taxes, do you? Any more than you would expect your personal physician to lie to you about your health. That is why I feel no small degree of annoyance when I observe the misdirection that comes from a segment of the financial industry that I believe should be more responsible – market-based financial advisors. To be fair, it may be that some of these untruths are founded in ignorance or lack of training. That is no excuse, however, because the profession to which they belong is highly regulated, and training and education are required before one can hang out a shingle and put an "open for business" sign in the window.

I am close to this issue because I'm a financial advisor who specializes in retirement planning. A lot of what I do when it comes to helping people with their financial problems is remedial in nature. That is, many times I find myself in the position of fixing someone else's mistakes.

When poor financial decisions are made because of wrong advice handed out by a financial advisor, you feel bad for the client. You hope and work to repair the damage and restore the client to financial health. You may also rightly feel a twinge of embarrassment because the mistakes of others, intentional or otherwise, can cast a shadow on an honorable profession in which the vast majority of those practicing are honest and competent.

LIES BROKERS TELL

Market-based financial advisors best exemplify the simple truth that limited tools and a limited scope of vision lead to limited and often inadequate solutions. In the 1800s, when peddlers of patent medicines hawked their bottles of elixir from the back of horse-drawn wagons, their favorite targets were the gullible who wanted to believe they could get a miracle in a bottle. For a couple of dollars they could cure a universe of ailments, ranging from toothache to tuberculosis. Of course, the claims were grossly overstated. The opiates these bottles contained were often potent and sometimes fatal when administered to children.

Brokers have a right to promote their businesses. After all, this is the American free enterprise system. But sometimes their approach to investors reminds me of these snake oil salesmen when they – how can I say this gracefully – *exaggerate* their capabilities? Oh, why try to put lipstick on a pig? These are ... lies; some of them are whoppers in fact. Here are a few of them:

1. Stock picking - This is the lie meant to convince you they possess the unique ability to pick a certain stock of a certain company that they know will do well. When asked how they know that this stock will do well and increase in value, the answer will usually have to do with such things as earnings reports, lines on a graph, and statistics on supply and demand within that particular market sector. All of this has a ring of authenticity and can be quite intimidating. The truth is, however, the stock picker has neither a crystal ball, nor the reincarnated brain of Nostradamus. They may get it right occasionally, but there is no way to do so on a consistent basis.

This sort of thing reminds me of a scene from the 1967 blockbuster film *The Graduate,* where Benjamin, a young college graduate, and the protagonist of the movie, is approached poolside by a friend of the family wishing to give him a literal "word" of advice about his future. The line is ranked as the 42nd most memorable lines in film history by the American Film Institute.

Mr. McGuire: I just want to say one word to you - just one word.
Ben: Yes, sir.
Mr. McGuire: Are you listening?
Ben: Yes, I am.
Mr. McGuire: Plastics.
Ben: Exactly how do you mean?
Mr. McGuire: There's a great future in plastics. Think about it. Will you think about it?
Ben: Yes, I will.
Mr. McGuire: Shh! Enough said. That's a deal.

It's kind of that way with advice from brokers. *"Don't ask for details. Just trust me. You see all these plaques on the wall here?"*
"Yes."

"Do you see all these computer charts and graphs here?"
"Yes."
"Well, you just run along now, and leave it all to me. Believe me, I can pick 'em."

What arrogance! My question is, where are those same people to be found when the market tanks and the stocks they picked don't fare well? I've had many victims of this con come into my office with broken portfolios and decimated life savings, needing help recovering from such errant advice.

Too many factors can affect a company's fiscal health, and do it so suddenly that it is nearly impossible to predict success. Sure, you can assemble data. You can put lines on charts, estimating profit and loss for years to come. But an overnight development could render all of those numbers irrelevant.

Some who claim to have mystic capabilities in this area of picking stocks that can't miss, fail to consider the most basic reason why this cannot be done – the human element. This facet of business is the one potential monkey wrench that can grind the gears of unstoppable juggernaut companies to a halt. A fickle public suddenly changes its mind and goes with a competitor.

Consider what happened to Kmart. It was the king of discount retailing in the early 1980s and Kmart executives thought the discount chain would always occupy that throne. Then along came Wal-mart, profits fell and stores closed. Kmart declared bankruptcy and was bought out by Sears Holding. Sears Holding failed to keep pace with internet shopping and now that respectable old mail-order retailer is almost out of business as this is being written. The point is, no one foresaw this. It just happened.

The human element is often irrational and, therefore, unpredictable. That's why stocks don't always perform as you anticipate they will. Confidence can melt into fear overnight, proving no one can pick stocks. No one. It's all guesswork. And like all guesses, sometimes the guesser gets it right.

What lures the unsophisticated investor is the desire to "strike it rich" by picking the dark horse at 30 to one odds and choosing a winner. Microsoft, for example, the brainchild of Bill Gates, was an IPO (Initial Public Offering) in 1986. Had you bought just a few shares and held it, your return would have been somewhere in the neighborhood of 35,000% by the spring of 2004. In other words, if you had put $10,000 into Microsoft and kept it for 18 years, you would have had a cool $3.8 million! But those who chase that rainbow, looking for the next Microsoft or Google, are in for crushing disappointment because we have 20-20 hindsight but are future blind.

Fundamental analysis has its place in helping us understand how the market works and the basic principles of individual stock movement. But it cannot predict the future...only the past. All the charts and graphs on Wall Street won't guarantee tomorrow. Investing strategies based on these may just as well be based on tea leaves or the lines in your palms.

2. Market Timing - Ah, here is another clever myth. The lie goes like this: "Why, yes, young man, we have sophisticated market analysis systems that tell when is the right time to get in and get out of the market. These computer programs track every little tenth of a second tick of the market's movement and, through some set of immensely complicated set of algorithms, they calculate with the speed of light just when we should make the move.

"You see these two large buttons here?"

"You mean the big green one that says, 'BUY' and the big red one that says, 'SELL'?"

"Yes. Well, our people study these graphs and computer-generated charts all the time and we

specialize in knowing exactly how to time the market so we buy low and sell high."

"What are all these blinking lights?"

"Oh, those...we really don't know. We bought that from the set of Star Trek. But I'm sure it somehow helps us time the market."

One of the reasons this works on people is that we are all psychologically wired to *want* to peer into the future – about everything. We even fantasize about what it would be like to know what's around the next corner. That's why palm readers and other fortune tellers stay in business.

So in the investment world, when a "guru" tells us he or she has such a magic wand or magic computer program that will enable us to buy low and sell high, we want to believe. But it just isn't so. No one can time the stock market. A market, any market, is, by its very nature, unpredictable. Just think back to the bursting of the tech bubble. Where were the market timers then? All on a Caribbean cruise? Sick with the flu?

If you choose to invest in the stock market, it should be done with the long term in mind. This is true especially if you are young, and in your "accumulation" years. Make regular contributions to investment funds that are passively managed. You will be the beneficiary of something called *dollar cost averaging*. Again, that means that when the market goes up, great! So does your account balance. When the market goes down, great! You are buying more of the cheaper shares with the same *regular* contributions. When the market goes back up, those skinny shares will fatten up and so will your portfolio. That eliminates the need to *time the market.* If you want the kind of adrenaline rush that such an activity will produce, however, a very glitzy city in Nevada would welcome your visit. I hear they have some wonderful entertainment there too.

Think about this: If you were able to get 312 people to believe you are a genius and can pick winning stocks, and if each one of those people gave you $100,000 to invest for them, you would have $31,200,000 to manage. The average broker charges 1.5% to manage investments, so that is an annual income of $468,000. Not bad! If the market goes south and you lose 50% of your clients' money (none of it is yours), you now only get 1.5% commission on $15,600,000, which means now you will only make $234,000 per year. A tremendous pay cut. I hope that doesn't mean you'll have to sell that yacht and the vacation home in the Florida Keys. Or worse yet, have to start mowing your own lawn.

The truth is, when the stock market swings wildly, as it has been inclined to do during the first two decades of the 21st century, there is no possible indication of what will happen next. If a market begins to slide, there is no way of telling how far it will drop and for how long, and vice versa with an upward swing.

But let me clarify something. While 80-plus years of research have proven that timing the market *accurately* with *consistency* can't be done, that doesn't mean some haven't hit it lucky. The key words here are "accurately" and "consistency." Some may even have good results for a long stretch, but sooner or later their streak ends.

One of the funniest lines I've ever read about this concept is in the book *Fooled by Randomness,* by Nassim Nicholas Taleb. He says that if you set an infinite number of monkeys in front of an infinite number of typewriters, one of them will produce an exact version of Homer's *Iliad* (the key word here is *infinite*). But then Taleb adds, "Now that we have found that hero among monkeys, would any reader invest his life's savings on a bet that the monkey would write the *Odyssey* next?"

3. We know what to look for. Speaking of lies, this is a big one. These are the people who tell you

their research has given them an *edge* over other brokers, and they know when the best time is to buy or sell an investment to get a better rate of return. Horsefeathers! Dalbar, Inc., which is a kind of Consumer Reports watchdog for the financial industry, produces some eye-opening statistics for the behavior of mutual funds. According to Dalbar, for the 20 years ending in 2009, the S&P 500 returned 8.2% annually, while equity mutual funds investors earned an average of just 3.2% for the same period. If it were really true that brokerage firms actually had special people who could know divinely just when to press the buy and sell buttons, then the Dalbar study would have shown brokers beating the market consistently over the 20 years of the study, when just the opposite was the case.

It's humorous to me when I occasionally run into brokers and ask them how things are going, and they tell me that they are "watching the market." When I ask them exactly what they are watching for, they don't really have an answer. They are just "watching the market." Whew! Now I can sleep better at night.

4. Track record investing – This is the one where they tell you that, while they *personally* can't pick stocks, time the market, or otherwise predict the

future, they have some really smart guys at the home office that manage large mutual funds and watch after large portfolios worth millions of dollars, and *they* can do it. And to prove it, just take a look at this fund here! See how much money it made over the last 10 years?

Well, what about that line of reasoning? Are there successful mutual funds out there that have good performance track records? Yes, a few. So what does that prove? Not much, and here's why.

This myth would have you believe that if a fund manager or a stock picker did well in the past, he or she will do well in the future. This myth suggests that past performance will reflect the future. There is a disclaimer on the bottom of the page you should pay attention to. *"Past performance is no guarantee of future results."* It means exactly what it says, folks. A manager's ability to pick stocks in the past has ZERO correlation with his/her ability to do so in the future. When you list the top 30 funds from 1989 to 1998, for example, they beat the S&P index by double digits.

A smart commission-based broker will point that out as proof that these people have it figured out. Why would you *not* want to pick one of these? But such streaks are anomalies. What they won't mention is that our list of funds that beat the S&P during the

1990s *failed* to beat the S&P in the decade that followed. In fact, none of the top 30 funds in the 1990s list were included in the top 100 funds of the 2000s.

There is also a "graveyard" of sorts for mutual funds that underperform. The data on these loser funds even disappears because those funds are quietly phased out ("killed off") and merged with other funds that did better. According to the Center for Research in Security Prices, University of Chicago, the total number of funds open in 2010 was 27,542. The total number of those phased out was 18,934. Do you see how that looking at *all* the data of *all* the funds – good, bad and average – would paint a truer picture of the track record? Do you get the sense, like me, that the data is being manipulated for the sake of profit? Did you know the average return of the worst 200 mutual funds that were closed ("killed off") in 2010 was *minus 77.7%?*

If you're like me, you don't pay much attention to warning disclaimers when you know they are just on the instructions to protect the manufacturer. (One of the silliest I ever saw was printed on a bottle of Windex©. The disclaimer read "Warning – do not spray in eyes.") But one label that bears paying attention to is at the bottom of any mutual fund

	1989–1998 (10 Year)			1999–2008 (10 Year)		
	Rank	% Rank	Annualized Return	Rank	% Rank	Annualized Return
Fidelity Select Electronics Port.	1	0%	29.67	2780	85%	-3.83
Fidelity Select Computers Port.	2	0%	28.54	2940	90%	-5.11
Fidelity Select Health Care Port.	3	1%	26.42	1443	44%	0.83
Fidelity Select Technology Port.	4	1%	26.18	2711	83%	-3.46
Seligman Comm. & Info Fund	5	1%	26.10	1495	46%	0.70
Janus Twenty Fund	6	1%	25.76	2036	62%	-1.02
T Rowe Price Science & Tech Fund	7	1%	25.60	3046	93%	-6.88
Alger Spectra Fund	8	1%	25.10	2001	61%	-0.88
AIM Financial Services	9	2%	25.07	3032	92%	-6.51
Fidelity Advisor Equity Growth	10	2%	24.91	2636	80%	-3.08
AIM Health Sciences	11	2%	24.88	NA	NA	0.00
Fidelity Select Banking	12	2%	24.49	2380	73%	-2.04
Fidelity Select Soft. & Compt.	13	2%	24.41	687	21%	3.60
Vanguard Health Care	14	2%	24.20	126	4%	7.92
Fidelity Contrafund	15	3%	24.04	877	27%	2.83
American Century Ultra Fund	16	3%	24.04	2647	81%	-3.15
AllianceBernstein Glbl Thematic	17	3%	23.85	2925	89%	-4.88
AIM Technology Fund	18	3%	23.78	3008	92%	-6.03
Franklin Growth Fund	19	3%	23.49	1589	48%	0.39
Fidelity Select Home Finance	20	3%	23.47	3018	92%	-6.21
Oppenheimer Main Street Fund	21	4%	23.40	2292	70%	-1.75
DWS Communications Fund	22	4%	23.35	3082	94%	-9.76
Fidelity Blue Chip Growth Fund	23	4%	23.17	2737	83%	-3.61
Wells Fargo Adv Larg Co. Grwth	24	4%	23.05	2797	85%	-3.91
John Hancock Regional Bank	25	4%	23.01	1801	55%	-0.28
MFS Growth Fund	26	5%	22.94	2842	87%	-4.17
Fidelity Select Retailing Port.	27	5%	22.45	2033	62%	-1.01
UBS Financial Sector Fund	28	5%	22.45	NA	NA	0.00
MainStay Capital Appreciation	29	5%	22.36	3019	92%	-6.22
Fidelity Select Financial Svcs	30	5%	22.24	2335	71%	-1.91
Top 30 Funds Average Return			24.41			-2.48
All Funds Average Return			15.52			0.74
S&P 500 Index			20.03			0.67
CRSP 1–10 Index			19.23			1.59
Total Funds 1989–1998			636			
Total Funds 1999–2008						3,278

For illustrative purposes only. Mutual funds data provided by CRSP Survivor-Bias Free Mutual Fund Database, includes funds that are U.S. Equity mutual funds. The S&P data are provided by Standard & Poor's Index Services Group. CRSP data provided by the Center for Research in Security Prices, University of Chicago.
Indices are not available for direct investment, therefore their performance does not reflect the expenses associated with the management of an actual portfolio.
PAST PERFORMANCE IS NOT A GUARANTEE OF FUTURE RESULTS.

document or advertisement, *"Past performance is no guarantee of future results. Investor may lose money."*

5. I have your best interests at heart. - This is a big one. Follow the money trail. Who pays them? Do you pay them for their services, or are they getting paid by a wire-house, brokerage firm, or a broker dealer firm. If you're not the one paying them, then they do *not* work for you.

Let me say that I believe most people in the community of financial professionals are well-meaning, hard-working people who do not intentionally set out to defraud you. But sometimes, stock brokers will put their interests ahead of yours. Here are some things to watch for:

Unauthorized trading is when a broker makes transactions on your behalf without your authorization. Typically, there are only two conditions under which a broker should make transactions on your behalf without your authorization. One is if you grant discretionary authority, and the other is when you give your broker expressed and detailed permission. If the broker makes a commission every time he moves in and out of a stock, regardless how the stock performs, the money trail may lead to overactive trading, or "churning" within the account. Check your statement. Has the same stock been bought and sold multiple times? Churning is a form of investment fraud and it is not likely to be in your best interests.

Just as a stock broker can fraudulently churn stocks in your account, a broker may also switch between mutual funds with excessive frequency, for no valid reason except to earn commissions. Another form of mutual fund sales abuse is selling various forms of loaded funds or Class B shares to clients who might qualify for Class A shares or be equally served by no-load equivalents.

Variable annuity sales abuse is prevalent enough for me to put it on your watch list. Variable annuities are complex and controversial investments. Sometimes salespeople present them as having the potential for growth of a mutual fund, possessing the security of an insurance instrument, and allowing you to invest in the stock market with a safety net. Well, some of that is true, but, as they say, the devil is in the details, and far too many people invest in these instruments without knowing the details and understanding what the wording in the contract portends. For example, you may be protected by a death benefit, but your variable annuity balance can be eroded by a falling stock market. Make no mistake.

You can lose your principle with these investment instruments. Have you been given full disclosure on the fees and expenses? Variable annuities (not to be confused with fixed annuities or fixed indexed annuities) are typically accompanied by fees that are so steep that it can take more than a decade to outperform more straightforward investments. All too often, the benefits are misrepresented, and the restrictive features and penalties aren't adequately understood.

If an investment advisor tells you that they have your best interests at heart but is reluctant to offer full disclosure and complete transparency, something tells me that there is a major integrity disconnect. In other words, they're not being straight with you.

6. *Markets are not accurate in pricing stocks. We can help you find which stocks are overpriced and which are underpriced.* Oh, this is a good one! Stock prices are set by market conditions that are open for everyone to see, analyze, and understand. The price you see on the ticker is based on all the measurable, knowable, and predictable information available. The only way to alter that determination is to somehow come up with *additional* knowledge ... *special* knowledge about the market that is hidden from the rest of the world. The only person I know who is that

prescient and omniscient is my 15-year-old son, who knows all. If you don't believe me, just ask him. While you're at it, perhaps you could ask him which stocks are overpriced and which ones are underpriced. Please pass the information along to me, because we have a little communication problem sometimes.

Unless you have access to an all-knowing teenager, or a crystal ball, you would not be in possession of any information about overpricing or underpricing of stocks.

7. We know what is going to happen next – either by looking at demographics or fancy pie charts. Just because people have a mid-life crisis does not mean we can use this to predict what will happen to the market next. Many gurus have tried to use demographic information to make predictions about what the buying habits of the baby boomers will do to the market. Most of the time, they fail miserably. But just make one correct prediction out of many and they are once again held up on a pedestal in the media.

John Bogle, the founder of Vanguard® Mutual Funds, is the first to admit that just because someone was able to beat the market last year, there is no scientific evidence, let alone proof, that they can repeat the feat. The retail investment world and the media have a vested interest in creating the illusion that you cannot figure out the market on your own. Their objective is to convince you that you need their special expertise and unique knowledge. If you don't fall for their Jedi mind tricks, they go out of business. That is why they spend hundreds of billions of dollars to make trillions of dollars. Then they are able to gamble speculatively with your money and get paid whether you make money or lose money.

Don't believe the lies. If you do, you're putting your retirement and the rest of your financial life in the hands of a system that has its own best interests at heart.

CHAPTER THREE

INVESTOR BEHAVIOR

Archie Karas (born Anargyros Karabourniotis in 1950) is probably the world's most famous gambler. Archie would bet on anything ... poker, pool, dice, cards. He has the record for the longest winning streak in gambling history where he turned $50 in 1992 into over $40 million by 1995. Happy ending? Nope. Later that year, he lost it all.

There's an old saying, "Nobody loses in Vegas." Mr. Karas may argue the point with you, but the meaning is clear. No one wants to remember the losses ... only the wins. People who play the stock market as if it were a roulette wheel tend to be that way with their investments too. They are proud to tell you about the times when they hit it big, but not so talkative about the times when they had their lunch eaten. Here is a list of 20 questions peeled right from the Gamblers Anonymous® website. If you can answer yes to more than 10 of them, you might have a problem. But just for grins, let's substitute the word "gambling" with the expression "investing in the market." It may reveal whether you have a problem in that area as well.

1) Did you ever lose time from work or school due to investing in the market? Yes/No

2) Has investing in the market ever made your home life unhappy? Yes/No

3) Did investing in the market affect your reputation? Yes/No

4) Have you ever felt remorse after investing in the market? Yes/No

5) Did you ever invest in the market to get money with which to pay debts or otherwise solve financial difficulties? Yes/No

6) Did investing in the market cause a decrease in your ambition or efficiency? Yes/No

7) After losing, did you feel you must return as soon as possible and win back your losses? Yes/No

8) After a win, did you have a strange urge to return and win more? Yes/No

9) Did you often invest in the market until your last dollar was gone? Yes/No

10) Did you ever borrow to finance your investing in the market? Yes/No

11) Have you ever sold anything to finance investing in the market? Yes/No

12) Were you reluctant to use market money for normal expenditures? Yes/No

13) Did investing in the market make you careless of the welfare of yourself or your family? Yes/No

14) Did you ever invest in the market longer than you had planned? Yes/No

15) Have you ever invested in the market to escape worry, trouble, boredom, or loneliness? Yes/No

16) Have you ever committed or considered committing an illegal act to finance investing in the market? Yes/No

17) Did investing in the market cause you to have difficulty sleeping? Yes/No

18) Do arguments, disappointments, or frustrations create within you an urge to invest in the market? Yes/No

19)Did you ever have an urge to celebrate any good fortune by a few hours of investing in the market? Yes/No

20)Have you considered self-destruction or suicide as a result of your investing in the market? Yes/No

Now, as ridiculous as it sounds, I would be willing to bet (pun intended) that some of you had a hard time staying under 10 yes's. Then *you might have a problem!* How we behave, or better put, how we misbehave, is by thinking we're in control, even when we're not.

My first time in Las Vegas, I found myself standing in the foyer of one of the big casinos. I saw slot machines and people working hard at colorful gambling stations. Noticing that all of the slot machines had three buttons on the front of the slot window, I stopped one of the workers to ask what the buttons were for. He proceeded to explain to me that each button would stop the slot wheel in front of it when pressed. He also told me the other button to the side of them started all three wheels spinning. But no one was pushing the button to start the wheels spinning. Instead, they would pull a lever on the side of the machine.

"Why is this the case? Why would they pull the lever and activate the wheels manually when they could accomplish the same thing with the push of a button?" I asked.

"It's all psychological," he said.

Seeing the confused look on my face, he continued. "They feel like they have more control over the outcome if they pull the lever."

I thought about that seemingly silly idea for a long time. But the more I thought about it, the more clearly I understood. It is strictly a matter of chance because there is no way you can actually affect the outcome. But if you can do something with your hand and be somehow actively involved in the process, you have the illusion of control. Psychologically, pulling down a lever gives you a feeling of control, even though the odds will never be in your favor at a slot machine.

As I mulled that over, a little old lady came up to me abruptly and screamed in my face, "That's my slot and you can't have it." I apologized for looking at it and backed off with my hands in the air. Then it occurred to me that it's much the same with some people and investing. The more actively they trade stocks, the more control they feel they have over the process. Making multiple trades is definitely activity, but I'm not so sure it qualifies as accomplishment. The only real winner in the stock-picking game is the brokerage house that charges a fee for the trades. The house always wins – as they say in Las Vegas. Frequent trading is usually counterproductive.

CHASING THE NEXT GOOGLE

There are those who love to operate on tips and suggestions they hear, either from a friend or workmate. Some will act on an investing tip they receive from the pages of one of the many investment magazines that have become so prolific as of late. They are in search of the next big winner. I call it the "chasing the next Google" syndrome. Some think that if they invest in the top five mutual funds they find listed on the internet, they can't miss. I actually know of a few who made investment decisions based on the rantings of the aforementioned comedian turned stock analyst who comes on TV with a bulb horn and a party hat. Whatever the case, those stories, like those of Archie Karas, usually don't have happy endings

Warren Buffet says that by the time you hear about an investment in the media, it is too late to get in on it. Most of the gains have already been made.

My advice is, if you're going to gamble, do it in Las Vegas. If we do not control our behavior when it comes to independently investing in the stock market, the market will surely control us and it won't be pretty. Chasing after the next Google or Apple is just not sound thinking. No sure thing is ever a sure thing until after it becomes a sure thing, and then it's too late. Slow and steady with caution and care are the best watch words.

Psychology plays such a major role in how we invest. Buy low and sell high is the mantra of a successful player in the stock market. Any novice will tell you that. But we aren't computers. Our emotions get in the way. It's human nature to seek pleasure and avoid pain. Here's what usually happens:

You watch a stock rise in value. You have the urge to buy it. But you're cautious. What if you're wrong? What if you buy the stock and it goes down and you lose money? Ouch! That would be painful. Wait and see if it is for real. Yep, the stock is continuing to tick up. Volume is up. The herd is moving in that direction, so you follow and place the order to buy. The stock continues upward. You are confident now. You knew you were good at this. In your enthusiasm, you even add to the position. But the next day the stock loses a few ticks. It's probably just a little profit taking, you tell yourself. No need to panic. You sleep well that night.

The next day, however, the first thing you do when the market opens is check the stock. You can't peel your eyes away from the computer. It's still going down. If you sell now, you'll lose. Ouch! You curse the crazy stock market for teasing you like this. Just as sure as you liquidate the position, it will go back up and make a fool out of you. So you hold. Yep, "You got to know when to hold 'em," you tell yourself. But you still keep checking the stock on your smart phone. It's dropping.

Now you're worried. You toss and turn that night. Your confidence of a few days before has turned into fear. The phrase "cut your losses" keeps crossing your consciousness.

"Cut your losses and live to trade another day," you say to yourself as you place the sell order. The stock drops even further after you sell, which serves to reinforce your decision.

The dominant emotion is now despair with a touch of nausea. You have run the gamut of emotions from caution, hope, commitment, confidence, enthusiasm, greed, denial, fear, panic, despair, and resignation.

It's a common story and one retold every day. The truth is that none of those emotions were rational. Rationality has nothing to do with it. Markets ride on emotion. It's all about feelings. When the market is going up, people feel rich. When stocks are going down, people feel poor. The truth is, as American economist Ben Graham once said, in the short-term the stock market is a voting machine – meaning that stocks will go up or down based on current events, what the spin doctors have to say about the news, natural disasters, or world events.

It is human nature to want to follow a herd. People are gregarious creatures and, like birds in flight, move instantly in the same direction and change that direction on a dime when something spooks the flock. Since the values in a volatile market represent people's whims and events that have no real bearing on the true value of companies the stock symbols represent, it is a mistake to make investments in and out of such stocks. Chasing the next big mother lode, like Google or Apple, is like playing the lottery. Your losses are simply feeding the machine, sort of like that slot machine in Las Vegas. Those chasing the next best sure thing will always be too late. You will always be buying high and selling low because of that instinctual urge to avoid pain and seek comfort.

Reading the above and recognizing it as truth are two different things, however.

Another psychological wrinkle that makes up our human nature is the one that tells us what we want to hear. We rationalize a lie to justify our destructive behavior.

"I will eat today and diet tomorrow."

"One drink won't hurt."

"I'll just gamble to get even and then I'll quit."

Another lie we tell ourselves is, "This time will be different from last time." It's impossible to overrule reality, folks. If we continue to allow our negative impulses to rule our investing behavior, it will negatively affect our retirement portfolio.

TO FAIL TO PLAN IS TO PLAN TO FAIL

Before we leave this topic, please allow me to offer a couple of suggestions. If you know going in that investing can be tricky turf, then go about it slowly and with deliberation. Take the emotion out of it. If you're in an emotional state and your finger is on the trigger, back away. Don't take any action. The opportunity, if it is one, will still be there tomorrow. Refuse to allow yourself to be pressured, even by yourself, to make a snap decision. Do you have all the facts? Have you given the matter due consideration? Have you asked for a <u>professional</u> opinion or two?

Second, it's always wise to operate with a strategy and a plan instead of going on a wing and a prayer. A defined strategy, especially one that involves your retirement, will include the following basic precepts:

Know where you want to go. It's like Yogi Berra said, "You've got to be very careful if you don't know where you're going, because you might not get there." Investing without having a goal is meaningless. Make your goal as real and as clearly defined as possible with respect to amount and time. That is, how much do you want to acquire with this particular strategy or investment, and how long should it take before this strategy produces the desired result? Put it down in writing. Using dates and figures makes it real. Mark that as Point B.

Know where you are. Point A starts with inventory. Figure your net worth, your income, and expenses. How much do you have in high-risk, medium-risk, and low-risk investments. Count everything. Is your furniture paid for? That's an asset. Estimate the replacement value and write that down. Calculate all sources of income. Do you own your own business and does your income vary from year to year? Use averages to give you something solid to work with. Do you have a strategy that involves placing regular contributions into an account? Make the amount you contribute realistic so you'll be motivated to continue making them despite the appearance of unexpected expenses.

Use the Rule of 100 as an investment strategy. Take your age and subtract it from 100. That is the percentage of your assets that should be invested with the degree of risk with which you are comfortable. It's called your *risk tolerance.* The rest should be somewhere safe. If you are already retired, prevailing wisdom is that your assets should be 100% safe.

Trusting in your instincts, or, as the popular expression goes, "going with your gut," is not always a bad idea. But it's not something you would do if you were, say, walking across a mine field. Personally, I would rather have a map to the mine field with a diagram showing me where each mine is buried. On top of that, I would want one of those bulky, protective suits I've seen worn by specialists on TV. Call me crazy, but I want all the protection and all the information I can get in today's volatile market. Investing is a complex endeavor. In today's market environment, it can also be dangerous. Seek the assistance of a competent professional who is (a) fully certified (b) fully trained and (c) completely competent. These three terms are neither synonymous nor interchangeable.

Finally, common sense dictates that you don't go to a foot doctor with a heart problem. If you're nearing retirement, you want to speak to a financial professional who specializes in retirement planning.

A BIRD IN THE HAND IS WORTH TWO IN THE BUSH

CHAPTER ONE

A PRUDENT WAY TO RISK

Believing lies can put one at great risk. A good example of this is what happened to Russian cosmonaut Vladimir Mikhaylovich Komarov. On April 24, 1967, Komarov became the first human to die in space flight when, because of engineering ineptitude and poor workmanship, the main drogue chute on his Soyuz 1 space capsule failed to deploy, and he plummeted to earth.

Soviet scientists were under immense pressure from their Kremlin bosses to beat the Americans to the moon, so they worked feverishly to keep on schedule. They took engineering shortcuts and bickered among themselves. Some in the program knew the Soyuz 1 spacecraft was substandard, but they lied to their superiors about its viability. They lied to Cosmonaut Komarov, omitting information he had a right to know since he was scheduled to fly the doomed craft. Because of the climate of fear that existed in the Soviet space program, many of the scientists and engineers responsible for the launch dared not postpone it. It might have given them time to work out the bugs and system design errors that surfaced just prior to liftoff. But they knew their necks would be on the Kremlin chopping block if they delayed.

Cosmonaut Komarov wasn't stupid. He was experienced in space flight, having been in orbit once before. He knew something didn't seem right about his anticipated flight. But when he asked questions, he was reassured by the engineers and scientists that Soviet technology was vastly superior to that of any other nation, most certainly the Americans, and that everything was just fine. He believed Soviet officials, who told him he would return safely to Mother Russia's soil and be hailed as a hero in a Moscow parade. Komarov was strapped into his spacecraft to the cheers and applause of many who knew, but still remained silent about the inadequacies of Soyuz 1.

The first sign of trouble came minutes after liftoff. Two solar panels were supposed to deploy and power the command module's new onboard computer system. Only one panel deployed, leaving the ship electronically crippled. This led to a navigational failure, which forced Komarov to resort to crude, line-of-sight techniques to re-enter the earth's atmosphere. According to the book, *Starman, The Truth Behind the Legend of Yuri Gagarin,* as the words of Komarov's final radio transmission crackled over the speakers inside Moscow's version of mission control, he could be heard screaming curses in Russian at the "people who had put him inside this botched spaceship." As his doomed spaceship hurtled earthward, he probably realized too late that his fate was sealed by his belief in the lies he was told – lies that put him at such great risk.

There is risk in all human endeavor. It isn't possible to completely avoid risk. Even if you choose to hide in your bedroom all day, some danger still exists. But some endeavors are riskier than others. For instance, the riskiest jobs in ascending order are: commercial fisherman, logger, airplane pilot, farmer, miner, roofer, sanitation worker, truck driver, and police officer. The very fact that risk can be measured and categorized in such a way lets you know that not all risk is equal. I was surprised to learn, for example, that it is more dangerous to be a commercial fisherman than it is to be a police officer. Did you notice astronaut isn't even on the top 10 list?

Likewise, when it comes to handling our finances, there is risk and there is *RISK!* Sadly, many incur risk because they believe the lies about investing – lies like the ones mentioned earlier in this book – that market prediction and accurate "stock picking" is possible. Believing those lies has cost many their fortunes. Blind trust can have disastrous consequences in your retirement outlook.

I'm not opposed to prudent risk, however. My advice is this: If you're going to be in the market, do it scientifically instead of putting your faith in the fairy tale that there are gurus out there who can time the stock market or computer programs that can pick winning stocks. If you're going to invest in the stock market, wouldn't it make sense to have a prudent, scientifically proven, time tested, Nobel Prize-winning way of doing it? Instead of placing our confidence in the "just-trust-me" hucksters, I much prefer using a methodology that has stood the test of time and was established on more than 80 years of academic research. If you have to trust somebody, I feel more comfortable trusting the academic community. They don't have a profit motive. Investing on the basis of findings made by scientists, mathematicians, and professors who have no "skin in the game," so to speak, leaves me with a lot better feeling about having all or part of my portfolio in the stock market. Unlike the scientists who misled poor Cosmonaut Kosmarov, these people are not pressured by any particular group to mislead you or sell you on their approach or investing philosophy. They are in it for the research alone. I call it landing on the "smart side" of the investing fence. I am not joking about the Nobel Prizes. The individuals who came up with the prudent market risk approach we will consider next are winners of multiple Nobel Prizes that have already been awarded and handed out.

THE CASE FOR A SCIENTIFIC APPROACH

"No risk, no reward" is a favorite saying among motorcycle daredevils, circus high wire walkers, and stock brokers. But, as I said earlier, not all risk is created equal. Some risk will never turn out well, no matter how much money you put on the line expecting a reward. There are some who think that if they embrace risk, they will be rewarded. They are convinced that higher risk will eventually pay off for them. In fact, they believe that there is a risk/reward ratio:- the higher the risk the greater the reward. They have converted the "no risk, no reward" proverb into "more risk, more reward." I'm sorry, but it just doesn't work that way. If you went outside in a thunderstorm, stood in the middle of a field with a lightning rod held aloft in one hand, what is your expected outcome? Best case scenario, you'll get cold and wet. Worst case scenario, you'll be front page news for the lightning strike and your bizarre behavior, and your obituary will appear on page six. No matter what, the outcome won't be pleasant. Risks don't guarantee good results.

The entire retail financial world is built on the premise that you can't deal with the market and its inherent risk on your own. This may be true to some extent, but to be quite frank, they can't do it either. So how do we structure our risk investments so we're not taking *unnecessary* risks, and still see acceptable rates of return? Academic research says that if we look at the right information, we can find where 91.5% of performance comes from. That is a huge number. "How did you come up with that?" you ask. Remember the Nobel prizes? The math has already been proven and we can actually measure it. Stock picking accounts for 4.6% of performance. Timing of the market is only 1.8%. Other factors, 2.1%. With results that low, you can see why there is no way that picking stocks or timing the market is a prudent way of investing. I would much rather go with 91.5%! The

91.5% is called asset allocation, and it has to do with how each type of investment is represented in your portfolio and how those investment types work together.

Asset allocation is widely spoken about and used in the retail financial world. So how do they still get it wrong? I'm glad you asked. The key to correct asset allocation lies in two main areas: correlation and asset classes. Most advisors of the investing world who talk about allocation don't use either one of these two investing concepts.

HOW DOES CORRELATION WORK?

Correlation is the relationship between two investments. If you truly want to protect yourself in a risk environment, you need to be diversified. The first key, and the cornerstone of diversification, is correlation. Are the investments you own going up and down in price at the same time? If all of your investments are going up at the same time, and when one crashes, they all crash, then you have exact correlation (same price movement). To have proper diversification there must be *opposite* price movement.

Instinctively, nobody wants to buy a stock that is going down. You only want to buy the ones going up. Your broker knows this and guess what they push to sell to you? All of the investments currently going up! But if you purchase all stocks going up, there is a good chance those stocks will all go down at the same time. A more balanced portfolio has stocks that move opposite of each other. So the key is to have one going up while another is going down.

But don't just stop there. If all you have is one going up and one going down, you aren't moving at all. You might as well put your money in a mattress. Yes, we need the opposite correlation but we need our entire investment portfolio value to trend up as some investments go down and others go up. How do we achieve this? *Asset classes.*

HOW ASSET CLASSES WORK

Asset classes are not the same as market sectors. Market sectors are the healthcare industry, manufacturing, finance, technology, etc. Asset classes are more specific and much more reliable. They are large USA stocks, small USA stocks, long-term government bonds, short-term government bonds, large international stocks, small international stocks, etc. If we study asset classes, we see that when the market goes up, we know how a particular class will do. When the market goes down, we know what a particular class will do. Of course, we don't know when the market will go up or down. But we know that it will. If, however, we know what to expect from our portfolio in different market environments, this makes investing easier and less stressful when the statements come in the mail.

Mathematically, we can allocate the right percentage of our portfolio to each asset class to get the highest expected rate of return with the least amount of risk – over time. This is not a guess. The math has already been proven several times and the Nobel Prize was handed out. So what is the catch? We don't know what the market will do next, and so the expected rate of return is over many years. Short term, the market may go up or down but long term (with enough time), the market will be up. So if you have time and you want to control risk, and you want an expected result, the right information gives you a prudent risk strategy. No stock picking, no timing the market, no trying to find someone who can.

"Why isn't the financial community doing this?" you ask. I asked the same thing many years ago. The answer wasn't surprising, but it was disheartening.

Retail financial entities are trying to make a profit. Not just a little profit, but a big profit. How they do this is by charging fees every time a transaction happens. You want to sell a stock? That's a transaction. You want to buy a new stock? That's a transaction. They ~~want~~ need you to believe and buy into the idea that a lot of transactions are not only the right thing to do, but beneficial to your investment account. More transactions = more money the retail investment firms make.

A strategy with opposite correlation and proper asset class mix doesn't need to be traded. There are no transactions, thus no fees for anyone to collect.

Simply put, the retail financial planning business cannot make as much money running your account in a scientific and mathematically proven way - no matter how many times it has been proven and no matter how many Nobel prizes have been handed out. - Even if it would be better for the investor.

IF YOU NEED INCOME, YOU NEED THIS!

While attending classes to become a financial advisor, my teacher said something that completely changed my life. It changed the way I look at financial planning as a whole, and how I have directed my career path to this point. As a result, I've had the privilege and the pleasure of helping many people.

I'm sitting in my class, taking notes, and the teacher says: "Someday, you will be sitting at your desk and one of your clients will be sitting across from you, telling you that they are ready to retire. They will tell you they need to start taking money out of their retirement accounts in order to supplement their income. And so, because you are a financial advisor, they will ask you, 'What's the best way to withdraw money so I never run out?'"

I have to tell you, this teacher had my attention. I listened with keen anticipation for the answer. My pen was poised above the notepad and I was ready to transcribe this golden nugget of information that would help all my future clients achieve true retirement success. I underscored the question, "What's the best way to withdraw money so I never run out?" I underlined the question with two red lines and had put a dash after it, eager for the answer. But my heart sank when I heard it.

"Just don't ever take out more than 5% and they will be all right," said the teacher.

"Really? That's it?" I nearly said out loud. "That's your nugget of wisdom for me to share with my clients that will ensure their success in retirement for the rest of their lives?"

I've always been good with numbers. I think in numbers. I'm always calculating this and running numbers for that.

"Your brain must be a terrible thing to live with," my wife, Teresa, said to me one day. I reminded her that she does, in a way, live with my brain every day. But I digress.

When this guy made that comment, my brain immediately went to work trying to calculate how that could possibly work. But to no avail. I couldn't get the math to add up. Then I did what you should never do in school. I raised my hand to ask a question. I'm not sure if he thought I was questioning his authority or his intelligence or what, but he began to verbally beat me up in front of the entire class for even questioning what he said. After all was said and done, his advice to me was to just believe it "because it works 90% of the time." So I shut my mouth and leaned back into my chair. But I couldn't get that 90% thing out of my head. I mean, if you were getting on an airplane, and I was checking your ticket at the door, and if I told you, "Great news! We have a 90% success rate in take offs and landings," would you get on the plane? I don't think so.

If I was your waiter at a restaurant and you asked me how the food was here, and I said, "Great news! We have a 90% success rate of not poisoning our customers," would you place your order, or would you beat a hasty retreat to the nearest exit?

You see, 90% isn't good enough. Especially when we are talking about rest-of-your-life money. So began my quest to find the answer to what I observed to be the number one concern in retirement. In planning sessions, I usually hear the question expressed in two ways: (1) When can I retire? (2) Do I have enough money to retire?

It's actually the same question, isn't it? People want to know how much money they can spend every month and never have to worry about running out. The key to having a successful retirement plan is, in a word, income. It's the income that you have, or don't have, in retirement that will determine your lifestyle. Without a doubt, there are other pieces to the retirement plan puzzle. We discussed some of them in previous chapters of this book. But the income piece is the keystone of the arch. Everything else hinges on it.

Anyone who bakes will tell you that a cake without eggs is not a cake. Leave out this one ingredient and you'll end up with a spongy substance lacking in taste. The same can be said of retirement income planning. A retirement income plan without the key ingredient – guaranteed income – just isn't a good retirement plan.

People ask me all the time, "Ron, what investments do you use in income plans?" I've seen just about every kind of investment you can name applied to income planning. Sometimes it reminds me of that old expression, "trying to fit a round peg into a square hole." As a registered investment advisor, I have access to all of them. My certification status even allows me access to investments that brokers and bankers cannot offer. But, when someone comes to my office asking the burning question that seems to be in the forefront of their minds – "How much money can I withdraw in the way of income without ever running out?" – they don't seem to be interested in projections or guesswork. They usually want to see guarantees.

RETIREMENT INCOME GUARANTEES

So let's look at a case study:

John and Mary Smith are both 59 and want to retire at age 62. John gets a small pension ($1,200 per month) and a small Social Security check ($900 per month). Mary gets a small Social Security check ($500 per month). They have three major concerns:

1. Their Social Security income and the income from their pensions will only cover daily expenses.

2. In order to maintain their current lifestyle in retirement, they need an additional $15,000 per year.

3. Both need to know they won't outlive their money.

Surveys have shown that the number one fear among those approaching retirement is not dying too soon, but living too long. At some point we all come to terms with the fact that we will die. But what if we out-live our resources, and are forced to spend those last years of our life in poverty? What if we lose our independence and our dignity, and become a burden to those we love? I'm always amazed at the lengths to which people will go to insure their homes and automobiles against the unknown, but they refuse to take steps to insure their lifestyle.

Think about it. If your income was insured so that no matter what happened, you still got your monthly check in the mail, how would that make you feel? Would you breathe a little easier? Would you sleep better at night?

This is why John and Mary Smith worked so hard all their lives to put money aside for their future. They wanted to make sure they have the money they need in retirement. They knew their pensions and Social Security wouldn't be enough. They cut corners and did without so that they could save for retirement. And they did a pretty good job. They were just a few dollars away from having accumulated $450,000 in their retirement accounts.

After careful analysis, we were able to determine that it would take $350,000 of that total to give them a guaranteed lifetime income for the rest of their lives that would ensure they would be able to enjoy the same lifestyle in retirement that they did before they retired. This left them with what I like to call an ECP (Emergency Cash Position) of $100,000. Not a bad little slush fund, eh? In fact, it would have to be a pretty dire emergency for $100,000 not to cover it.

So we take the $350,000 and use it to fund "Advanced Income Solutions," our proprietary retirement income planning program that represents a culmination of all of my years spent searching for the best way to take income out of a retirement savings account without depleting the principal. The investments I use have three common denominators. They are *guaranteed, insured,* and *interest bearing only.*

Guaranteed means your money is always there. Insured means that even if these banks go out of business, you will still get your money back. Interest bearing only means that your money is never "at risk" in the market. You have reputable companies putting it in writing that they will pay you every month, for as long as you live (guaranteed), the amount agreed upon that matches your wishes. Now you have a plan you can live with.

I can hear what you are asking, "Ron, this sounds too good to be true. What is the downside?

What is the catch?" The downside, or catch, is this: these are very boring, very dull investments. They are not sexy; they are not flashy. If the market goes up a bunch, you won't ever see it. But, if the market goes down a penny, it won't affect you. Boring, dull, interest bearing accounts.

My retired clients absolutely love being boring and dull. Why? Because boring and dull is also predictable and transparent. Boring, dull, predictable, and transparent is comforting, and it increases their peace of mind – something that is *huge* in retirement planning. It means less anxiety, less stress, less blood pressure medication, and more fun. Hence, more time to focus on things more important than money.

Comparing Apples to Tacos

CHAPTER THREE

PICKING AN ADVISOR

The metamorphosis of a caterpillar into a butterfly reminds me of the transition from the workaday world to the new life of retirement. In elementary school, we kids studied this curiosity of nature. One day this earth-bound worm just stops munching on leaves and wraps itself up in a cocoon. The next day, or so it seemed, what was once a slug became a beautiful butterfly with gorgeous, feather-light wings.

You want your transition into retirement to be just that smooth and painless. The day will come when you wake up on the first morning of your retirement, glance at the clock, and remind yourself there's nowhere you have to be. Go ahead. Yawn, stretch, sip your coffee, and read the newspaper. It's finally your life. It no longer belongs to an office, the boss, or some self-imposed routine. You are free. The last thing you want now is a cloud of financial uncertainty hanging over your head like the one hovering over those who failed to plan properly for this day.

Nature tells the caterpillar when to stop thinking like a worm and start preparing for its future. One day, for no apparent reason, the caterpillar changes its routine and, on some instinctual cue, seeks a safe place under a leaf and begins wrapping its body in silk. We humans, however, sometimes need prodding to help us realize it's time to plan ahead for the big changes in front of us. Unlike the caterpillar, we humans will likely need some help with our metamorphosis. Of course, when it comes to planning for retirement, you can certainly go it alone if you wish. You could also try do-it-yourself auto repair. In both cases, it may turn out okay for you, especially if you have some skills and training. But for many, many others, trying to go it alone in either category may prove to be a disaster, for both their finances and their automobiles. Mastering personal financial planning isn't easy and requires many hours of research and education. Even if you had the aptitude and acquired the training, the time factor may be a killer – especially if you want to get it right.

WHOM CAN YOU TRUST?

From time to time, when I'm called upon to speak before a group about financial planning, I like to open it up to questions, just to see what's on the minds of the people out there. This is one way I keep attuned to the public pulse. You certainly won't find out what people think by burying your nose in trade journals or studying charts and graphs. Just by listening, I've discovered the main reason why most people put off selecting a financial professional to help them with their retirement planning is because they don't trust anyone.

I can understand this one. Quite frankly, with all of the market unsteadiness, economic volatility, idiots trying to steal peoples' life savings, and just plain bone-heads giving stupid advice, it's no wonder some folks struggle with how to choose an advisor these days. What really curdles my milk is to pick up the newspaper and read of the fat cats on Wall Street mucking things up with underhanded financial dealings that are so shady not even government investigators can catch them until it's too late. When global financiers like Lehman Brothers, Goldman Sachs, Morgan Stanley, and Merrill Lynch get caught with their pants down, it bends your trust needle back to zero in a hurry. As the dust settled after the 2008 stock market crash, we began to see just how fragile some of the large investment banks were. These were the Wall Street big boys considered "too large to fail." With all the brain power at their disposal, they were still unable to conduct their affairs properly. Nearly all of these banks were caught up in the same subprime loan mess, making one bad decision after another until the house of cards began to waver and then list to one side. Some were bailed out, some were bought out, and others simply faded away. Main Street would never feel the same again about Wall Street.

Then there was the Bernie Madoff scandal. When the former NASDAQ chairman confessed that Madoff's wealth management business was really the most elaborate Ponzi scheme in history, a shocked nation watched in disbelief. How could such a thing happen? Who's minding the store? How could one man bamboozle $64 billion (that's billion, with a "B") out of so many unsuspecting patrons? We watched the evening news videos over and over of an innocent-faced Madoff looking stunned and puzzled as they arrested him and hauled him off for fraud. Also stunned and puzzled were the 4,800 clients who put their trust in him.

So it is no wonder, then, that John Q. Public began scratching his head, wondering whom he could trust with his money.

LOOK FOR A FIDUCIARY

Start by looking for an advisor who is a fiduciary. Fiduciary – now that's a word you don't hear tossed around a lot.

The word "fiduciary" comes from the Latin word, *fiduciarius*, meaning "to hold in trust." The word connotes *a legal or ethical relationship of trust between two or more parties.* The root word of "fiduciary" is the Latin *fides*, which means true. Other related words that share the same root are "fidelity," "bona fide," and "confidential," all of which have to do with trust and faithfulness.

In the financial world, fiduciaries are ones who pledged to look out for the interests of their clients and always put those interests ahead of their own. The advice of a fiduciary is always client-driven, never profit-driven. The best type of fiduciary is a Registered Investment Advisory Firm (RIA). This simply means that financial professionals within this firm made an official pledge, at the risk of losing their licenses and hence their livelihood, to always place their client's interests ahead of their own. They are audited every year by state and/or federal government securities regulators to ensure this happens.

You can't stop there, however. You also need to work with someone who can understand your financial goals and execute your wishes. In other words, someone with the capacity to think like you do. If you're like most folks, you are trying to follow a certain path for your retirement. You need someone who knows where that path is going and who can help guide you down it. What you don't need is someone who tries to pull you down a different path, simply because it is a direction with which *they* are most familiar. Let me give you an example:

In my RIA firm, we specialize in preserving wealth and utilizing wealth to create a supplement to income that will never deplete the assets. So when someone comes into my office seeking advice, the first thing I want to know is what's on their mind. How do they think? What are their notions about money and finances? If we can match our thinking, then we might be able to work together. If we don't match, there is no need to go further. I can't help them.

Here is the process I go through to figure this out: First, I ask them to pretend that all their money was cash and that it was stacked up in their living room, waiting to be invested somewhere. Obviously, you can't just leave it in the middle of the living room floor. What attribute would they want the new investment into which they are placing their money to have? Second, I ask what they would want next out of their money. Third, I ask what else is important to them about their money. Usually, when all is said and done, I find that my clients and I share the same core beliefs and this promotes a good working relationship. Here is a list of those priorities we usually have in common:

Safety
Growth/Income/Returns
Taxes/Fees
Liquidity

Safety of the assets is my number one concern. Growth is the second most important concern. When you put them in that order – safety *then* growth– that equals *wealth preservation.*

If you put growth first, then safety, that equals wealth *accumulation.* I can certainly accommodate that, but it's not my specialty. I would usually encourage a "growth first" person to work with someone else, and I am happy to offer recommendations. I specialize in wealth *preservation,* not wealth *accumulation.* I don't disregard growth; it's second on my list. It's just not my number one.

As you can see, matching up your beliefs about money and finances with those of your advisor is a critical step in making sure your advisor can help you down the path you prefer. Another big piece of the puzzle, and one that should figure prominently in your search for the right advisor, is ascertaining exactly how they are compensated. If you are paying them, then they work for you. If a brokerage house, or some other major firm, is paying them, then they don't work for you. It's as simple as that. They work for someone else.

Next, ask about experience. How long has the candidate for your business been advising clients? You probably don't really want to be a new advisor's guinea pig.

Also, ask what other services they offer. Can they really provide a well-rounded approach? Or is their focus so narrow they only know one path? Remember the old expression credited to Abraham Maslow: "If the only tool you have is a hammer, you tend to see every problem as a nail." What other services do they offer?

Service is important in financial planning. How often will they meet with you to discuss your progress? The financial landscape changes constantly. Your needs and your thinking may change too. You need to meet with your advisory firm at least once a year, maybe more often than that, to keep pace with these changes.

Lastly, do you like this person? What is your gut telling you about this person? Don't ignore your gut instinct because it's mostly right in measuring trust. Feelings, after all, are facts. Do you feel that you can trust this individual to be an advocate for you in this important area of life?

KEEP AWAY FROM MY NEST EGG!

CHAPTER ONE

PROTECTING YOUR NEST EGG FROM PREDATORS

It seems that in nature, nest eggs are easy pickings for predators, which explains the way some birds behave with their nests. Robins, for example, will sometimes make their nests in the craziest of places, but don't ever try to move a robin's nest, or even touch it, or the bird will abandon it. Somehow they just know. There is one documented case of a robin that built her nest in a working construction crane. Despite all the noise and motion, the mother bird incubated her eggs and raised her babies there, only abandoning the nest when her hatchlings were big enough to fly.

In another case, a robin built a nest in the car of a moving freight train. As the car moved from place to place along the tracks, the bird and her offspring went with it. As the mother builds, she is apparently memorizing all the features around the nest. When those features are disturbed, or if well-meaning humans move the nest in an effort to protect it, the bird will abandon it, sensing that it has been discovered and disturbed by predators. When a storm dislodged a nest containing four baby blue jays, the people who found it put it back where it came from, but the mother never returned.

As we edge closer to retirement, our nest egg will hopefully become more developed and more valuable. As in nature, this is when we need to be the most alert for predators. As the theme of this book suggests, those who would put your life savings at risk don't always operate in back alleys, or have sly countenances. Nor do they speak and dress like the stereotypical con artist. White collar thieves can come in all manner of disguises, even that of a reputable businessperson.

One couple with whom I met (we will call them the Wadsworths) were victims, not of any outright scheme or illegal con game, but they were victims nonetheless. They watched their retirement savings grow during their working years and now, as they approached their mid-60s, they planned to retire. Their family owned business was reasonably successful. They managed to provide their children with a comfortable home and a good education. Now, they calculated, they had enough to retire. They figured that if they were careful with their expenses, they could maintain the comfortable lifestyle to which they had become accustomed, and enjoy a worry-free retirement in their sunset years. Because they were self-employed, neither of the Wadsworths had pensions. They would rely on the money in their investment account, combined with their Social Security income, to see them through.

Then, in 2008, the Wadsworths experienced a financial train wreck. They watched nearly half of their hard-earned savings evaporate virtually overnight when the stock market fell more than 700 points in one day. Neither the husband nor the wife had ever concerned themselves much with the details of their investment account. "After all," Mr. Wadsworth would say later, "isn't that why you have financial advisors?"

"Just stay the course," their financial advisors told them. "The market always comes back." So, not knowing what else to do, the Wadsworths stayed put. Perhaps it was because they were impressed by the glass tower building and the marble floors. Or it could have merely been that they were trusting souls who felt it was rude to ask questions. But they would explain later that they felt betrayed by the ones in whom they had placed their trust. They thought they were in good, professional hands, but those hands fumbled the ball and offered no explanation and no apology, other than the bland consolation that the pair weren't the only ones to be affected by the market crash. They were given some hollow illustration about "all the boats going lower with an outgoing tide." Meanwhile, the Wadsworth account continued bleeding.

"I understand that the tide goes out and comes back in," said a frustrated and justifiably angry Mr. Wadsworth. "I get that. But what do you do when the ocean disappears."

Along with the financial erosion experienced by this couple came the inevitable dimming of their once bright retirement dreams. When I encounter situations like this, I'm reminded of my first aid training in the Army at Fort Lee, Virginia. The first thing to do, I learned, is to stop the bleeding. This was financial triage. My first order of business was to save what remained of the Wadsworths' savings and regroup. The most severe damage done here was the loss of principle to the account. After stabilizing and protecting their assets, we put a plan in place for a steady rebuilding of their wealth. There was no magic silver bullet here. Some sacrifices had to be made. The couple decided to postpone retirement and continue working for four years, giving them time to accelerate the rebuilding of the account. At the end of five years, they would exercise a lifetime income option that would, as things turned out, pay them more than they were planning on before their account suffered the loss. All in all, it was a relatively happy ending for these folks. Since they were both in good health and enjoyed their work, postponing their retirement for a few years was not too objectionable. They were relieved to have a plan in place that would guarantee them safety and a suitable income they couldn't outlive. They were comfortable with the safety and growth potential of the new plan, and they said they felt as if they dodged a bullet.

Were the Wadsworths victims of fraud? Not really. They were victims of either one of two things: (1) gross incompetence on the part of well-meaning but uninformed and misguided financial professionals who should have known better than to have placed so much of their clients' assets at risk when they were close to retirement, or (2) maliciously insensitive money handlers who were so greedy for commissions and fees that they purposely misled their clients into dangerous investing turf. Either way, their nest egg was raided, and the result was the same.

A TIME FOR CAUTION

As more and more baby boomers transition from the workaday world into retirement, fraudulent activity is on the rise. The Securities and Exchange Commission (SEC) reported that in 2011 it filed a record 146 financial-fraud enforcement actions against investment advisers and companies. That's an increase of 35% percent in just three years. In one case, three senior executives of an Ohio-based finance company were charged with orchestrating a $230 million fraudulent scheme that involved 5,200 investors – many of them elderly. Under the guise of loans, company executives allegedly diverted investor proceeds to themselves so they could enjoy lavish lifestyles.

"These executives looted... and exploited unsuspecting investors who trusted the company to prudently invest their funds," said Robert Khuzami, director of the SEC's Division of Enforcement. "To add insult to injury, they squandered the stolen funds on such extravagances as multiple homes, a private jet, a yacht, and more than 40 classic and exotic cars."

A few large investment management companies were also on the SEC chopping block in 2011. In one case, the SEC alleged securities law violations in connection with the offer, sale, and management of mutual funds.

"All financial firms and professionals — including large mutual fund providers — must be vigilant in accurately describing the risks of the products they sell to the public, especially the widely-held mutual funds that are the bread-and-butter investments of retail investors," Khuzami said.

It is obvious why the elderly are targeted. They have more money, for one reason, and, as a demographic class, they are viewed as being more naïve. A report from the Center for Retirement Research at Boston College observes that the elderly are less able to make effective financial decisions without assistance. Dementia and other types of cognitive impairments increase with age. The Center pointed out that one-fifth of people between ages 71 and 79 are impaired, and half of those between the ages of 80 and 89 lack competency to some degree. Even if you feel completely competent right now, it just makes good sense to protect your nest egg by building safeguards into your retirement plan. It couldn't hurt. Here are some suggestions:

(1) Keep it simple. Multiple accounts are more difficult to keep up with than just a few. Seek advice on the most efficient and practical way of combining funds.

(2) Limit access to your accounts. Cap the amount that anyone, including yourself, can withdraw from your accounts without verification.

(3) Pay attention to your passwords. Change them often. Have a foolproof system for remembering them and share it with as few individuals as possible.

(4) If you have sensitive documents that would reveal private financial information, invest in a document safe (less than $200 at any large office supply store) and a shredder. Never dispose of them in the carry-out trash.

(5) Work with an advisor who is a fiduciary - someone legally required to put your best interests first.

(6) Select a trusted younger family member with whom you can share your financial information. Take them into your confidence in case you need to call upon them for help.

(7) Give some thought to putting a portion of your assets into a trust and naming a younger, trustworthy family member as co-trustee.

FINANCIAL ABUSE OF THE ELDERLY

There is no question the elderly have targets on their backs. According to a study conducted by MetLife, older Americans lose nearly $3 billion every year to financial abuse. Half of it is perpetrated by strangers. Sadly 34% of this abuse is at the hands of relatives and family friends and exploitation by the business sector accounts for the remaining 16%.

Women are twice as likely to be victims of elder financial abuse as men, according to the study. Most victims lived alone and were between the ages of 80 and 89. Most of the schemes and scams were perpetrated by men between the ages of 30 and 59. The majority of the scams were pulled off during holiday seasons.

The study revealed the most diabolical financial crimes committed against elderly persons involved situations where the con artists knew their victims and the fraud typically took the form of forged checks, embezzlement through bank accounts, stolen credit cards, and coercing older victims to transfer assets. Jobs pulled off by strangers were often of a more violent and aggressive nature, such as purse snatching, breaking and entering, burglary, and muggings.

Here are some ways the elderly can protect themselves against such attacks:

(1) Don't isolate yourself. You may live alone, but surround yourself as much as possible with friends and others of your age group. Those who live isolated lives are more vulnerable.

(2) Put your financial affairs in order using some of the same suggestions made earlier in this chapter.

(3) Choose service providers carefully. Have someone you trust screen applicants. Only employ caregivers whom you trust implicitly.

(4) If you live alone, don't open your door to anyone who isn't trustworthy. If it is important, they will wait until you have a companion with you.

(5) Keep jewelry and other valuables out of sight. Don't invite trouble by flashing cash, jewelry or credit cards. Keep such things in built-in home safes or safety deposit boxes. If there is nothing worth stealing visible in your home, you are less likely to be targeted by thieves.

(6) Stay clear of those asking for handouts, especially those with substance problems. They are more likely to prey on you

(7) If you don't have deadbolt locks, get them. Lock all your doors and windows at night.

We must remain watchful for threats that pose risk to our retirement nest eggs. Whether these threats involve market volatility, fraudulent advisers, or just unforeseen circumstances, like the sudden loss of employment, the better informed we are, the better prepared we will be. Most predators don't announce their presence.

VULNERABLE 401(K) PLANS

According to the U.S. Department of Labor, even 401(k) plans are not immune from plunderers. In 2010, the Department of Labor's Employee Benefits Security Administration (EBSA) initiated what they call the Contributory Plans Criminal Project (CPCP) to combat criminal abuse of contributory benefit plans. Who are they after? Primarily those who have authority over plan assets and misuse it to line their own pockets, both on corporate and personal levels. These people may try to use payroll contributions to enrich themselves personally, or they may misapply employee contributions to cover business expenses. I found no statistics to tell me exactly how much of this goes on, but the fact that a government agency would be formed to nab the perpetrators is cause enough for alarm. The CPCP primarily aims its spotlight at 401(k) plans, but the project is also interested in fraud involving contributory health plans. Investigators have uncovered instances where white-collar thieves, operating as third party service providers, gained access to plan funds and siphoned off money for their own personal gain. Other abuse has taken the form of identity theft and credit card fraud.

Some of the deception or trickery uncovered by investigators boggles the senses. In one Tennessee case, a third-party plan administrator was sentenced to a 12-year prison term and ordered to repay $20 million after pleading guilty to 29 counts of embezzlement from employee benefit plans. Third-party plan administrators are a common thing. Large companies hire third-party administrative companies and pay them handsomely to manage plan investments. In this case, however, the fees weren't enough. This embezzler, who was the Chief Executive Officer of such a firm, oversaw the collection of contributions for the retirement plan. But instead of placing the money with the custodian as he was supposed to do, he spent the money on a lavish lifestyle, even buying an expensive Japanese art collection, among other frivolous things.

Most of us trust our employers, but you have to be careful. In 2010, the EBSA announced the filing of lawsuits against 24 employers who diverted more than

$7 million of workers' retirement contributions to prop up their own businesses. Typical of the many smaller violations was the Lexington, South Carolina, steel factory that withheld $7,554 from employees' paychecks over a 2½-year period, but didn't place the money into their retirement accounts. I wonder if the owners of the steel mill knew just how much the government frowns on that sort of thing. Don't worry. They found out.

Believe it or not, I know some folks who don't even open their quarterly 401(k) statements. It could be blind trust, or it could be lack of interest, but I know of others who zip open the envelope, glance at the balance, and then toss it in the discard pile as if it were a mail circular. To some, retirement may be so far in the future they just assume everything's okay. Why worry about it? If I could borrow the megaphone for a moment here, dear reader. *IT'S YOUR RETIREMENT PLAN!!* It *matters* how you have it invested. It *matters* how it's being looked after. We can't be complacent, folks. Please check your quarterly statements and make sure your nest egg is not under attack, and that all of your contributions are accounted for.

What's that? You don't understand all of the information on your statement. Excuse me? You say you tried to read it and it all looks like Egyptian hieroglyphics to you? No problem. One thing my business partner, Kip Nussbaum, and I love to do in our office is walk folks through those statements. I'm sure that your financial advisor will be happy to do that for you too. Education is the most important service people in our profession can provide. Before we leave the subject, here are 10 warning signs (thanks to the U.S. Department of Labor) that your 401(k) nest egg may be under attack:

1. 401(k) account statement is always late or arrives at irregular intervals.

2. Account balance doesn't appear to be accurate.

3. Employer fails to transmit your contribution to the plan in a timely manner.

4. A large drop in account balance not explained by normal market conditions.

5. 401(k) statement doesn't reflect contributions withheld from your paycheck.

6. Investments on your statement aren't what you authorized.

7. Former employees aren't getting benefits paid correctly or on time.

8. Unusual transactions, such as a loan to the employer or plan trustee.

9. Frequent changes in investment managers or other plan consultants.

10. Your employer is experiencing severe financial difficulty.

"IF IT SOUNDS TOO GOOD TO BE TRUE..."

The main reason why Bernie Madoff is now a household name and one that will live forever in infamy is because those who fell for his scam believed in something too good to be true. When every other brokerage firm in the nation showed losses, Madoff's accounts continued to gain. That should have been a major clue. And it was to a few. But most of his dupes wanted to believe the unbelievable. They convinced themselves the unrealistic returns he was producing for the unwitting participants in his Ponzi scheme were legitimate, even in the face of evidence to the contrary.

Just say the first part of the following time-honored maxim and you will probably know the second part. "If it sounds too good to be true... it probably is." Over time, averaging in all the good years and the lean years, the stock market has experienced an annual increase of approximately 9%. If someone is promising you more than that, they had better have a good explanation for it – one that will stand up to close scrutiny and every background check you can run on the one making the promise.

One couple with whom I'm acquainted lived frugally all their lives. They owned a modest home and were in their late 70s when they were approached by an insurance agent representing what appeared to be a legitimate company. The man was friendly and charming, and the couple saw nothing in his dress or demeanor that would indicate that he was out to take advantage of them. But they were about to be victims of what is called a "promissory note scam."

In this scam, the masterminds often stay "in the shadows," so to speak. That is, they don't approach the victims personally. Instead, they find honest but naïve independent life insurance agents to work for them, enticing them with promises of large commissions. The agents are supplied with sales materials that look legitimate, and they usually don't know the information is false and misleading. A promissory note is a form of debt, like a loan a company may issue to raise money. They are a legitimate tool for raising money, business to business. The investor loans money to a company in return for the company's promise the loan will be repaid, with a specific interest amount over a specific time. In general, promissory notes are not sold to the general public, however. In this case, the promissory note was printed on rich, thick paper. It looked quite official to the older couple. But the issuing company didn't exist.

The hook was the promise of a 16% return within a year. The couple took the bait because they lived through the high inflation days of the 1970s and had fond memories of their money earning that much at the local bank. They sunk $25,000 into the deal – approximately one-fourth of their life savings. They knew they had been bamboozled when they tried to check on their investment but reached numbers that had been disconnected. The crooks used a portion of the money to pay the insurance agent his commission, but they absconded with the rest. The insurance agent lost his license but couldn't pay the couple back. The matter was turned over to the authorities, but every trail to the perpetrators was a dead end.

Always be suspicious of anything that is too easy, too quick, and too lucrative. If there is one principle that reigns supreme in the world of finance and investing, it is this: Everything is a trade off. Higher interest rates are usually accompanied by a longer term of investment. That's why a five-year CD yields more than a one-year CD. Shorter term investments with great liquidity are usually accompanied by lower rates of return. Finish these statements.

There is no free_____.

You can't have your cake and _____.

PROTECTING YOUR NEST EGG FROM THE TAX COLLECTOR

At first I thought it was a scrap of paper, or maybe a leaf, skittering toward me in the parking lot. Then, as the breeze brought it closer, it took on a more familiar look. It was a $20 bill! As I picked it up, my first inclination was to find the person who lost it and return the money to its rightful owner. Honest! That was my first thought! But the more I played out that scenario in my mind, the more I began to realize just how unrealistic that impulse was.

"Would the owner of a $20 bill please contact me immediately?" Right.

So I put the bill in my pocket, giving it a good home with a couple of other presidential portraits, and reflected on the windfall (literally) as an appropriate compensation. This little wind-borne gift, I reasoned, was fate's way of paying me back for all the times that I lost money without knowing it, leaving it for someone else to find. After all, what goes around comes around, I mused.

Finding money like that is a happy little surprise that I believe most, if not all of us, have experienced at one time or another. If you don't believe me, try this the next time the conversation lags at a dinner party. Ask around the table, "What is the largest amount of money you've ever found?" Nearly everyone will have a story. One friend said when he was in college and down to his last nickel, he found a $100 bill on the floor of a hallway. The most common find is a $5 or $10 bill in a coat pocket, or an old purse. I call it "found money."

FOUND MONEY RESCUED

I love to see the expression on our clients' faces when we discover "found money" hiding in plain sight on financial documents, especially tax returns. When prospective clients come to our office for a free consultation, I do very little talking. My usual custom, especially on first interviews, is to follow the golden habit I picked up from one of my many mentors, Ron Perkins – listen twice as much as you talk. You can't solve a problem unless you first identify it, right? By listening, you sometimes find things you weren't even looking for.

The woman in my office told me that she had income from investment accounts that she wasn't spending. She just didn't need it. She was reinvesting it each year. She said that what bothered her most was having to pay so much in *taxes*. She was particularly bothered by the fact that she was paying the maximum tax on her Social Security checks each month.

Let me pause for just a moment here and fill in some background information on the matter of paying taxes on Social Security. You may hear different versions of this, but the story goes that when President Franklin Delano Roosevelt signed the Social Security Act into law, he was asked if he would ever tax the benefits. He is said to have adamantly responded, "I will never tax Social Security." While FDR was alive, SS benefits were not taxed. But in 1983, President Ronald Reagan signed the Social Security Amendments of 1983 into law. This new rule provided that 50% of SS benefits would be taxed if a single taxpayer earned $25,000 or more, and a married couple filing jointly earned $32,000 or more. President Bill Clinton, in 1993, signed legislation that raised the taxation to 85% of benefits for single beneficiaries with incomes over $34,000, and couples earning more than $44,000.

Please bear in mind that these taxes are levied on *reportable* income each year. Wait a minute! You mean there is income that is *not* reportable? Yes, and we will get to that in a moment. First, here are categories of income that the IRS considers to be reportable:

- Ordinary income (of course)
- Income from pensions
- Income from market investments
- Income from bank CDs

What the IRS *does not* require you to report is *tax deferred* income, such as gains on annuity balances, for example. Will you pay taxes on the money that is earned inside an annuity eventually? Yes, of course. Either you or your heirs will. But we used this little provision in the tax laws to help our client in this case "find" some money by keeping it out of the clutches of the taxman. Like I said, one of the indefinable rewards of my profession is finding money for people. This client had never had anyone talk to her about these provisions. Needless to say, she was elated. Here's how it worked. Imagine a sort of "time line" with the following entries:

- 2007 tax return.

- On line 8-A of the tax return, there was $25,000 of taxable interest from accounts she never intended to touch.

- She also had a pension in the amount of $12,000 and Social Security of $12,000.

- Out of the $12,000 Social Security, 85% of that was taxable, or $10,200!

- Her adjusted gross income that year was $47,200 and taxes were $5,718.

- The following year, 2008, we eliminated the reportable interest on the return from the previous year, by moving the money generating the taxable interest into a tax deferred account. The pension was still $12,000.

- But now look at the taxable portion of Social Security - ZERO! Why? Because the Social Security taxation threshold was not met.

- Her adjusted gross income that year was $12,000 and taxes that year were $171 and a potential tax savings of $5,547!

- The following year, in 2009, she would have to start drawing from her IRA ($6,000) because she was now 70½.

- There was still no tax on Social Security because the Social Security threshold was not met.

- Her adjusted gross income was $18,000 and taxes were $728.

- So in 2009, she was able to take $6,000 in additional income and was still able to reduce her federal income tax by $4,990 over 2007.

"Oh happy day!" she giggled, when it sunk in that she was saving that much in taxes and she would no longer have to pay taxes on her Social Security, a notion that always irritated her as being patently unfair. Then I reminded her of a favorite saying around our office:

Intaxication: Euphoria at getting a refund from the IRS, which lasts until you realize it was your money to start with.

TAXES – A DIFFICULT PUZZLE PIECE

One of the reasons our firm has staff members who specialize in the field of taxes is because every situation is different. Seeking the advice of a tax professional is always a prudent action.

Recently, a couple with whom we were working made it known they wanted to retire early. Most of the puzzle pieces of their retirement plan fit together easily, but not so the tax piece. They weren't sure how much of their income they should budget for taxes. All too often, taxes are not factored into a retirement plan at all, an omission that can come back to haunt you. At other times, it is simply factored in incorrectly, which can cause its own brand of trouble. If you overestimate taxes, you may delay your retirement unnecessarily. If you underestimate them, you could derail your retirement by running low on income and having to go back to work. The reason why it's difficult to estimate taxes perfectly accurately is because it's a little like aiming at a moving target. Will tax rates stay the same? I doubt it. Will tax laws stay the same? I doubt it. Many things about the tax code could change over the entire course of your retirement. So while we can't nail down this aspect of retirement planning as accurately as we'd like, there are many areas where we can make broad-brush decisions that may enhance retirement income by not paying taxes unnecessarily. Choices made in the planning stages with tax consequences in mind will provide us with a platform accomplishing the goal of reducing taxes as much as possible in retirement.

401(K) AND IRA WITHDRAWALS

Both 401(k) plans and IRAs (Individual Retirement Accounts) are designed to allow your savings to accumulate during your working years so they can produce an income stream for you in retirement. While you are contributing to these plans, you are in the *accumulation* phase of life. When you stop contributing into these plans and begin taking money from them, you enter the *distribution* phase. Paying attention to how you withdraw this money is crucial because of the tax consequences. These are tax-*deferred* accounts, not tax-*free* accounts. Withdrawals from traditional 401(k) and IRA accounts are taxed as ordinary income and can be subject to a 10% penalty if you're below age 59½. With a 401(k), one way to avoid that 10% penalty is to make sure you're older than 55 when you leave the company. If you qualify for that exception, you may not want to roll your 401k into an IRA for that reason until you reach 59½.

When you turn 70½, you'll be required (by the IRS) to take out required minimum distributions (RMDs) from your IRA, whether or not you want nor need the money. Sorry, but that's the law. The amounts you are required to withdraw each year are based on your life expectancy (according to IRS tables) and are fully taxable. The government isn't stupid. They don't mind deferring the taxes. They know they will get more in the long run. And they *will* get their cut. But with *Roth* accounts, you pay the taxes up front and no taxes on the back end. Think of it this way: You pay tax on the seed, but not the harvest. With Roth accounts, the withdrawals are not considered taxable income as long as you're over 59½ and the account has been open for at least five years. Even if you don't meet those qualifications, you can still withdraw the sum of your contributions at any time and for any reason without tax or penalty. Can you see where understanding that little wrinkle in the tax laws could save you a boatload of money in taxes?

Remember, Roth withdrawals make the most sense in a year when your income tax bracket is higher than normal. Otherwise, it's best to delay them as long as possible and let those tax-free earnings accumulate.

YOUR PERSONAL RESIDENCE

According to IRS law at the time of this writing, you are allowed to sell your home when you retire and not pay tax on the gains as long as they don't exceed $250,000 ($500,000 if owned by married couples filing jointly). At one time, once you turned 55, you had a one-time option of excluding up to $125,000 of gain on the sale of a primary residence, but that rule changed in 1997. Age is no longer a consideration. There are some caveats, however. Requirements to qualify for this exclusion are:

- You must have lived in the home as your primary residence for at least 2 years (the use test), and
- You must have owned the home for at least 2 years (the ownership test), and
- During the 2-year period ending on the date of sale, you must not have excluded gain from the sale of another home.

I'm not advocating this as a strategy, but I am aware of one situation where a couple (he was a home builder by trade) bought land every two years and built a new home on it. As soon as they moved into the new residence, they would sell the old home and use some of the tax-free money from its sale to start building the next one. The obvious downside to that strategy is constantly moving around. And what if land values nosedive? But it is an interesting example of someone using tax laws to one's advantage.

PENSIONS, TAXES AND ROTH CONVERSIONS

If you are one of the fortunate few who have a pension, you are likely aware that the payouts of such arrangements are taxed as ordinary income. That means that they are subject to progressive tax rates, just like your salary, but without the FICA portion. In other words, the more you earn, the higher the rate. So when you are chiseling out that tax piece (not paying FICA), you can consider it a pay raise.

There are some possible negative tax consequences to taking your pension early. If you take your pension while you're still working, the extra income could bump you into a higher tax bracket. If you need the money, then you need the money, but be alert to this possible landmine. Taking your entire pension or a portion of it as a lump sum will mean paying taxes on the amount taken. Remember, you can defer taxes by rolling the lump sum into an IRA or another qualified retirement account.

There may be some circumstances where it becomes attractive to convert your traditional retirement accounts into Roth accounts. Don't forget that you will pay taxes on the amount converted. Roth conversions can be tricky, so it is best to consult with a competent professional before making the move. Here is a rule of thumb I use. It is usually not a good idea to convert to a Roth if you have to use money from the account you are converting to cover the taxes you will incur. Also, a primary reason for going with a Roth conversion is to reduce taxes. It is not a smart thing to do if that mission is not accomplished. What if you would be in a significantly lower tax bracket when you eventually withdraw the money from the account? Then it may be better to leave it as is.

A couple of things to think about: Roth IRAs are not subject to RMDs. Roth 401(k)s, which are gaining in popularity in the American workplace these days , *are* subject to RMDs. What it boils down to is this: Will you be able to reduce taxes over the long run? Can you afford to pay the taxes on the conversion with money outside the converted account? If the answer to both those questions is yes, then it may be a practical thing for you to do.

INTEREST INCOME

As most everyone knows, interest from such things as savings accounts, certificates of deposits, and bonds is subject to ordinary income tax. When you restructure for retirement, these accounts are usually the first investments you want to house inside a tax-deferred annuity. If you choose to reduce taxes by using federal tax-free municipal bonds, be sure to pick ones from your own state. In many cases you can avoid state taxes as well. Be sure to check the bond's rating. Some municipal bonds these days carry a high risk of default. And beware; the tax-free interest still counts toward the Social Security Threshold.

STOCK DIVIDENDS

Anything written and approved by Congress is subject to change. Before 2003, dividends from market-based investment accounts were taxed as normal income at the taxpayer's regular rate. Regular income tax rates are progressive – that is the more you earn, the higher the tax rate, which, as this book is written, can be as high as 39.4%. When President George W. Bush was elected, he argued that taxing dividends was double taxation. Why? Because the corporation already paid taxes on the earnings and then used post-tax money to pay dividends. The Jobs and Growth Tax Relief Reconciliation Act established something called "qualified dividends" that would be taxed at a lower rate. Turns out that most dividends are "qualified dividends," and the tax break turned out to be a real tax break for stock market investors, since their gains would no longer be taxed as ordinary income. This was enacted as a temporary measure with an expiration date of December 31, 2008, but was later extended through 2012. As this paragraph is written, it is based on exceeding a level of income. Plus, additional taxes apply in the form of a Medicare tax.

AVOIDING TAXES IS LEGAL

There's an old joke that goes, "What is the difference between tax avoidance and tax evasion? – About 20 years."

Most Americans, at least those with whom I am acquainted, don't mind paying their fair share of taxes. They just don't want to pay a dollar *more* than their fair share. Like Arthur Godfrey once said, "I'm proud to be paying taxes in the United States. The only thing is – I could be just as proud for half the money."

You can blame the Civil War for income taxes. In July 1863, right around the time of the Battle of Gettysburg when the nation was draining its coffers to pay for more rifles, bullets, cannons, and ships to fight the Confederacy, President Abraham Lincoln and the Congress enacted a temporary income tax to pay for it all. It wasn't much at first, but the toe of the tax collector was in the door. In 1864, the rate was 5% on income between $600 and $5,000; 7.5% on income $5,000–$10,000; and 10% on income $10,000 and above. It took a constitutional amendment, the 16th, ratified in 1913, to make income tax a permanent part of American life. The first Internal Revenue Service Tax Code was 400 pages long. Over the years, the IRS code grew exponentially as the laws multiplied and became more complex. Today's code book has over a million pages and is twice the size of Tolstoy's *War and Peace*. But every conceivable provision (read loophole) that exists is printed there. You just have to know where to find it, understand it when you read it, and know how to apply it. Who do you think pays the most in taxes – the informed, or the uninformed? Right...the uninformed.

Most retired folks are on fixed incomes. Higher taxes can diminish their quality of life and reduce the legacy they planned to leave to their heirs. During your working years, things were pretty straightforward. All you had to do to determine how much you were being taxed was to look at your paycheck stub. Even if you were self-employed, you certainly knew when you filed your tax returns. It's a different story when you retire. There are hidden tax landmines. The key to avoiding them is knowing where they are and understanding how to diffuse them.

CHAPTER THREE

PROTECTING YOUR NEST EGG FROM INFLATION

At the education workshops I conduct from time to time, I will sometimes reach into my pocket and pull out a dollar to make a point. I ask those in the audience to imagine that the bill represents their life's savings.

"This represents your entire retirement nest egg," I will say. "All the money you worked so hard to save. Here it is! Your IRAs, your 401(k), your investments, your pension, your Social Security, the equity in your home... everything! This is all you are going to be living on now that you have stopped working. How many of you want to do all you can to protect this?"

Every hand goes up.

"But let me tell you what can happen to this money," I continue. "Every year the nest egg is eroding, little by little. Not because you've bought a vacation home, or taken a trip, or helped your grandchildren go to college. This money has simply evaporated because of inflation."

We save all of our lives to *preserve* money, not to waste it.

Inflation is a silent and persistent thief. It tears our money away from us in small bits and pieces and, except for a few periods in history, it is a constant eroding feature of our economic landscape that we have come to accept as one of its components. Aside from a few years back in the 1970s when it burst forth in double digits and had to be subdued and put back in its cage, inflation was a tame monster, averaging approximately 3% annually since World War II.

In 1973, back when men wore pastel polyester leisure suits and women wore miniskirts, the nation experienced what was dubbed an "oil shock." Whether the gasoline shortage was real or manufactured doesn't matter. The lines of automobiles at the fuel pumps were real. The effect to the economy was real. Inflation jumped to 7.7% annual rate that year, and then climbed to 9.1% in

1975. By 1979, inflation soared to a jaw-dropping 11.3% and topped out at 13.5% in 1980.

For those earning fixed interest, the theft was most deceptive. They were accepting the gift of double-digit interest rates from the right hand of inflation, while the left hand robbed them blind. True, banks were paying 16% interest on savings accounts, CDs, and money market accounts, but they were charging 20% on loans. It was a good time to be in a cash position, but prices were going through the roof. The spin off was a declining stock market and a recession that followed in the early 1980s.

Any way you spin it, inflation is an economic varmint that is always lurking. According to some economists, the nation is vulnerable for another attack of runaway inflation in the future. Steven Cunningham, director of research and education at the American Institute for Economic Research, says that roaring inflation is a phenomenon caused by errant economic policies, many of which are enacted by politicians trying to help the economy.

Those who predict another run like the 1970s of double-digit inflation explain that efforts to boost a failing economy are likely to backfire when the Federal Reserve pumps money into the economy, which in turn builds up bank reserves. This creates a bubble that will eventually burst when banks begin lending money too freely once again.

The slack economy that defined the decade from 2000 to 2010 kept the inflation rate reined in. But if you begin to notice prices rising at a brisker pace than usual, it may be an indication that inflation is loose again. Check the price of a jug of milk, a dozen eggs, and a restaurant meal. Those are better indicators than the price of gasoline or the cost of a new home in an unstable economy. I read recently where a Forbes magazine financial writer's order at a fast food restaurant cost $10. All he ordered was a three-piece takeout chicken dinner with coleslaw, baked beans, and a drink. That means that a family of four will pay $40 to eat out at Big Daddy's Original Recipe Fried Chicken Heaven. There are causal factors for those kinds of prices, and they may, or may not, be a warning of run-away inflation. We will all find out about that together.

On October 24, 1978, President Jimmy Carter delivered a speech to explain what his administration was doing to combat raging inflation. Here's an excerpt:

"If inflation gets worse, several things will happen. Your purchasing power will continue to decline, and most of the burden will fall on those who can least afford it. Our national productivity will suffer. The value of our dollar will continue to fall in world trade."

Inflation continued to rise after the speech and would not abate for another two years. No matter what your view is of inflation, it's a good idea to prepare for it by planning for it. Add at least 3% to whatever your estimates are of your income needs. Add at least 3% to your estimate of what your expenses will be. If inflation doesn't pose a problem, you can consider the budgeted but unneeded money a bonus. No matter your view, it's still prudent to keep a sharp eye out for inflation. It's nobody's friend.

CHAPTER FOUR

PROTECTING YOUR NEST EGG FROM YOU

*"The only true wisdom is knowing that
you know nothing. ∼ Socrates*

When my daughter was five years old, she was full of questions. What five-year-old isn't, right? But with Shawnie, it was a running dialogue.

The most important lesson I ever learned about being successful personally and financially, I learned from her: "I do not know."

Only when we can recognize that there is "stuff we don't know," will we grow in knowledge. How can we learn something unless we first acknowledge that we do not know it? When I began thinking about writing this book, my main goal was not merely to educate, but to make a difference. If there is one thing

I've learned in life, it is that you cannot force people to learn. You can be a fountain of information, a veritable river of knowledge that you impart with skill and enthusiasm, but if there is no "impartee" to receive it, you are confusing talking with teaching. The education process is like a radio broadcast. Without a receiver, nothing really happens, does it?

WHAT WE DON'T KNOW CAN HURT US

My father, Jim Tetley, had no way of knowing that a highway accident would end his life at age 44. Had he known that this would happen, he would not have allowed the life insurance policy that covered him to lapse. Had my parents known that the 401(k) at work was invested in extremely volatile mutual funds that were subject to major loss, he would have invested them more safely. They were recovering from the shock of the 1987 market crash when he died. They didn't recognize that their life savings were severely at risk because they just assumed that the professionals to whom they entrusted their accounts knew what they were doing. They were never exposed to education about such things. Had he been, however, I am sure things would have turned out differently financially for my mother; my father was not the type to arbitrarily close his mind to things.

The worst kind of ignorance is when someone has a mind that is made up and doesn't want to be confused by the facts. The foundation of learning lies in knowing what you do not know. As I thought about the questions that came from my 5-year-old daughter's mouth, I reflected on how much we are capable of learning if we will first acknowledge that there are things we don't know. I suppose this is one of the reasons why I latched on so fiercely to the idea that most people who make financial mistakes, like the ones my parents made prior to the 1987 market crash, make them because of a lack of education.

I began to discover in my career as a financial advisor and retirement planner that no matter how true a thing is, and regardless of how passionate one is about imparting that truth, the effort to do so goes no further than the barriers that people tend to put up to learning something new. Which is why, dear reader, if you can just say those four words, I DO NOT KNOW, an entire world of new concepts will be open to you – new ideas about wealth building, wealth preservation, and worry-free retirement that you never knew existed. Some of these concepts and ideas have the power to impact your financial future in ways that are more profound than you can imagine. They have the *power* to do so. That doesn't mean you will put any of these concepts into place. But it does mean you're open to learning them, and that's a start.

LEARNING TO LEARN

I have noticed this about intelligent children: They are intensely involved with life. They have a love affair with learning. When I was in elementary school, and even for a while in high school, I was shy and kept to myself. When I began to come out of my shell, it was like that metamorphosing caterpillar mentioned previously. Once I poked my head out of my cocoon and caught a whiff of all of the excitement life had to offer by not being such an introvert, I emerged hungry to experience it. I observe my own children, and their gusto for life, and I hope they continue to embrace learning new things.

We expect things in nature to make sense. Why should it be any different in the world of managing our finances? When I conduct workshops, I love to see the heads begin to nod and the knowing expressions begin to appear on the faces in the audience when something I am pointing out connects and resonates with them. It's like seeing that proverbial light bulb appear over their heads as they say to themselves, "I get it!" They are excited to learn something new and different that will either (a) keep them from losing money, or (b) provide them with more money. Some will even volunteer the acclamation, "That makes sense!" which I have to tell you is my favorite response of all when I am teaching. Why? Because regardless of how worthwhile, smart, wise, lucrative, intelligent, profitable, and prudent an idea is, if it doesn't make sense to us, we won't act on it. At least we shouldn't.

Experts, in the learning process that children undergo in school, make the observation that the most intelligent children expect answers to make sense to them. They instinctively check their answers, and even their thoughts, against the matrix of common sense before they write or orally give an answer. Less intelligent children don't do this. They see things differently. They don't expect answers to make sense. They just write or say what they are given and told is right without performing a "does-this-make-sense" check.

To the more intelligent children, a problem is a picture with a piece missing; the answer is the missing piece. More intelligent children, the experts found, take their time to see, feel, and mentally grip the problem, allowing the answer to drop out the bottom. They differ from the "answer-grabbing" children who see a problem as an order to start running at top speed, in an unknown direction, to an unknown destination.

They dash after the answer before they have duly considered the problem.

An interesting comment on this was made in the July, 1958 issue of *Scientific American*, in the article "Profile of Creativity," where two students were compared as follows:

"Here are Elaine, the answer-grabber, and Barbara, the thinker, at work on the problem 3/4 + 2/5 = ?

Elaine (adding tops and bottoms, as is her usual custom): Why not 5/9?

Barbara: 5/9 is less than 3/4. She saw that since 2/5 was added to 3/4, the answer would have to be bigger than 3/4; so 5/9 could not be it. But this went right over Elaine's head.

Elaine: Where's the 3/4?
Barbara: In the problem!

Yet I doubt that any amount of explaining could have made Elaine understand what Barbara was saying, far less enable her to do the same kind of thinking for herself.

The poor thinker dashes madly after an answer; the good thinker takes his time and looks at the problem. Is the difference merely a matter of a skill in thought, a technique which, with ingenuity and luck, we might teach and train into children? I'm afraid not. The good thinker can take his time because he can tolerate uncertainty, he can stand not knowing. The poor thinker can't stand not knowing; it drives him crazy."

What I thought was so fascinating about that story, was that it illustrates how we don't see things that are right in front of us sometimes because of preconceived notions and attitudes toward problems. When it comes to handling our finances intelligently and profitably, we can cost ourselves thousands upon thousands of dollars by following the herd instead of asking ourselves, "Does this make sense?" If the answer to why we have our hard-earned fortunes invested where they are is, "That's where I was told to put it," then we need to stand up, walk out of that room, and enter the room of "does-that-make-sense" thinking.

Expressed digitally, the answer to the problem the girls were working on, $3/4 + 2/5 =$, is 1.15. Because Barbara wasn't thinking the problem through, she quickly added the two numerators (top numbers) and the two denominators (bottom numbers), and hastily wrote her answer as $5/9$. Either she didn't have the lesson on adding fractions with uncommon denominators, or she didn't pay attention during that class. But it is a classic example of running to the wrong conclusion because we *think* we know something that we *don't know* and failing to use the "does-that-make-sense" test. The more intelligent girl simply said to herself, "Wait a minute. The correct answer can't equal less than one, because both fractions, if I think of them in terms of percentages, 75% and 40%, add up to more than 100%."

IT'S HOW YOU LOOK AT THINGS

Every day, I help people who are very smart, even highly educated, who come to me after having made a serious mistake with their finances. Some of these people have PhDs. I even have one client who is actually a rocket scientist. Many of these folks are in professions that require them to make rational, intelligent decisions. But let me illustrate why it is that people, educated or not, intelligent or not, make mistakes in the handling of their finances.

> # Intelligence is not what you know, but what you do when you don't know.
>
> ~ Piaget

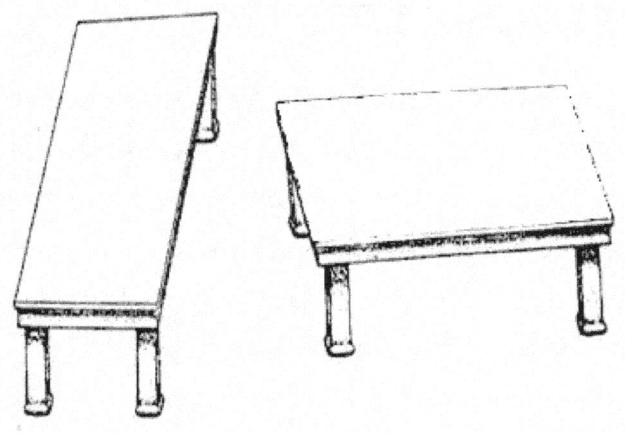

WHICH TABLE IS LONGER?

Your immediate impression is that the table on the left is longer. But you already know because of the context of the subject under discussion, that they're both the same length. Go ahead, measure them. I did. They are both the same length. You are looking at and, without further knowledge, believing an illusion. But even after you process what you know, after having proven it to yourself, you are still *inclined* to believe in the illusion. Why is that? It's because we have learned to rely on our vision to tell us the truth, the whole truth, and nothing but the truth. Seeing is believing, isn't it? Eighty percent of our learning is visual; we use our other four senses for the rest. We trust what we see. Scratch that ... we trust what *impression* our eyes convey to us.

If we can't always trust our vision, which is hardwired, what makes us think we can trust our judgment, especially if we are making financial decisions – an area in which we have no training? How many of our visual impressions are biased by preconceived notions, making us see what we want to see? Similarly how many of us "see" what we want to "see" when it comes to our money?

When I first entered the financial advisory profession in 1994, the stock market was on a roll. For a few years in the latter half of that decade, market-based financial professionals could do no wrong. Any recommendation they made was a winner. But then again, you could throw a dart at the financial page of the *Wall Street Journal* and bought whatever it landed on, and you would have done well.

"Risk tolerance? What is that? There is no risk if every horse you bet on wins." That was the mood of the American public. A kind of euphoria set in. The Soviet Union fell and Communism was disappearing from Eastern Europe. Trade opportunities expanded. This was also the decade of the computer. Technology was king. America couldn't get enough of cellular telephones, laptops, and desktop computers. All of this equipment had to be manufactured, of course, and a vast computer hardware and software industry sprang up.

Inflation was low. Profits were high. Unemployment was virtually unheard of. The Dow Jones Industrial Average, which had stood at just 1,000 in the late 1970s, hit the 11,000 mark in 1999. The talking heads who analyzed the market on television saw no end to this cornucopia. They predicted a 20,000 Dow (one guy said as high as 40,000) within a few years. All of this added substantially to the wealth of Americans. Homebuilding was on a roll. Auto dealerships couldn't keep expensive cars on the lot. It was the boom that would never end...until it did.

It is now referred to as the "market crash of 2000." The NASDAQ fell from 5,132 in March 2000 to 1,108 in October 2002. The Dow peaked at 11,723 on January 14, 2000. By October 9, 2002, it was at 7,286.

The loss of wealth was numbing for the country – almost S8 trillion. How could everyone have been so mistaken? No one saw it coming.

Over the years, I have become quite accustomed to helping people recover from financial mistakes, but after the market crash of 2000, I felt like a first responder at a disaster scene doing financial triage. Because I specialize in safe-money investing strategies, I am happy to say that none of my clients lost any money in that crash, or the one that occurred in 2008. Safe-money investment strategies always become more attractive after a market crash. Sometimes it takes a health scare, like a mild heart attack, or a mini stroke, to make some people start paying more attention to their eating habits and exercise routine. It was like that with many who came to my office following those two market catastrophes. They were shocked at how quickly they could lose so much from portfolios that they thought were in good hands. Many placed their trust in brokers who were no doubt all smiles when the market was soaring, but now, when they answered their telephones, only offered hollow clichés like: "These things happen," "you're not the only one," and the old standby, "hang in there; it will come back."

Many investors were justifiably angry and felt betrayed. These losses were not just numbers on paper. For many, especially those nearing retirement, these lost assets represented their security and independence. Now, worried and feeling vulnerable, many were eager to listen to suggestions on alternative investing strategies – retirement plans that would offer them complete safety with reasonable growth and options for lifetime income if desired.

COGNITIVE ILLUSIONS

With visual illusions, it is easy to demonstrate misconception. Take the illusion on the next page for example. It *appears* there is a bulge in the middle of the checkerboard. The truth, however, is that all the lines are perpendicular. There are no curves in the illustration. Only squares with right angles. With *cognitive* illusions, however – the ones where the illusions are in our minds – misconception is much more difficult to demonstrate. These cognitive illusions follow the same pattern, however. Those folks who lost so much of their money in the market downturn of 2000 and 2008 were operating

under the illusion of safety, when they were actually at risk. (Go ahead…take a credit card and make sure those middle lines are straight).

What are some of those cognitive illusions that may have influenced investing mistakes? Here are a few:

Bonds are always safe. People sometimes move into bonds, thinking they are safe from market volatility. It doesn't work that way anymore.

"Wait a minute," you may say. "My broker would tell me to get out of bonds if they weren't safe." Really? Would the owner of an automobile dealership tell his customers to go down the street to a competitor because the competitor's cars scored higher on a *Consumer Reports* crash test? Not likely. You are more likely to hear, "Stay right here and we will take care of you."

Here's a pretty safe bond. It's called the Bellwether Bond (30-year US Treasury bond). Back in 1981, it earned 13.5%. If you locked it in then, you'd be great. At this writing, the yield on this bond is an anemic 2.79%.

Until 2008 the game was: when the market was going good, you put most of your assets in equities. When the market heads south, you put most of your assets in bonds (as a defensive posture). In 2008, all of that changed. At a time when the market was losing and you were supposed to be moving into bonds, the bonds began to lose as well; 58.5% of bonds lost money in 2008. Some bonds aren't even around anymore. Some companies that made bonds their business vanished. Anyone heard of Lehman Brothers?

All annuities are safe. Annuities are like cars. There are good cars and bad cars. Fixed annuities are safe. Fixed indexed annuities are safe, as the word "fixed" seems to indicate. Variable annuities are anything but "fixed." Variable annuities are market investment instruments with an insurance wrapper. Both gains and losses are possible with this type of annuity. You can start out with $100,000, and a month later have only $80,000 in your account ... or less, depending on how your stocks perform. Are these vehicles protected by a death benefit? Yes. But let me ask you a question. Let's say your variable annuity has a $110,000 death benefit. How much money can you pull out of an annuity that is worth $80,000? $80,000. Can you pull out the death benefit? No. How do you get the $110,000? Die. We see people make this mistake all the time (not the dying part). They believe the lie, that as long as their account has life insurance, somehow their money is safe. Again, how much money can you pull out of an annuity that is worth $80,000? $80,000.

You need Long-Term Care Insurance. That's the illusion. The truth is you should never buy *traditional* long-term care insurance. Before you throw this book across the room, let me first of all say that I think everyone should protect themselves from the expenses associated with long-term care or receiving care in a nursing home. But there is more to the story. A long-term care insurance agent may point out that 43% of all people who are age 65 and older will need some sort of long-term care. And that is true. But they leave the statistic at that. The illusion causes you to imagine that it's probably a coin toss as to whether you will be one of those who wind up in a nursing home. What they don't tell you is that of that 43% who end up needing long-term care, more than 80% of them are over the age of 80 when they do. That changes things dramatically. You could be paying for long-term care for decades before you may or may not use the benefits. What happens to all of those premiums if you never use the policy? They don't go to you or your family if you die. There are other ways to protect yourself from these expenses, especially if you have assets that either have too much at risk or assets that are safe but earning you little or nothing in the way of interest. Have you ever heard of a *Combo?* No, not the one where you get a drink and fries with the sandwich It's insurance industry's nickname for products that combine life insurance and annuities with long-term care coverage. With the annuity combo, imagine a legal pad with a line drawn down the center. Part one is a regular fixed annuity, nothing fancy, that gives you a guaranteed minimum return, of say 3%. It's a conservative program, money that you don't have to have immediate access to in its own right. If you never need long-term care, or if you "die with your boots on" as the saying goes, then the money goes to your family. Prior to that, it grows tax deferred and can always be annuitized, or turned into a lifetime income stream. If you DO need long-term care, then this product acts as long-term care coverage with the benefit payout typically equal to three times the amount of the annuity. To make the math easy, say you purchased a $100,000 LTC/annuity, it could potentially pay long-term care benefits of $300,000, with your initial $100,000 used up first. There are three or four versions of this product on the market now, and that is a broad brush example. The life insurance version works on the same principle but the machinery works differently. The point is that there are *alternatives* to traditional LTC policies that, unless you had them explained to you, you wouldn't know existed. The reason why traditional long-term care insurance hasn't been accepted enthusiastically by mainstream America in the past few decades is because it is a "use-it-or-lose-it" proposition. If you don't use the policy on which you have paid premiums into for all those years, then that money is gone. If you keep the policy for years, and then it becomes too expensive to maintain (yes, the rates with traditional LTC insurance go up from time to time), then you will likely let the coverage lapse, and, again, you get none of that money back. So these combination policies were developed as an answer to that problem.

Combos aren't for everybody. Some companies require a physical, for example. You may not qualify due to poor health. Others may not have $100,000 to invest. But if you have the resources just sitting around in say, a CD, earning 1% interest, and if long-term care is a concern, then it may be suitable for you.

Without market risk there can be no reward. This illusion has been around a long time and it plays perfectly into the hands of those who profit from the misconception. The truth is that it's possible to have rewards from the stock market without actually being invested *in* the stock market. Have you ever heard of a *fixed indexed annuity* (FIA)? They're relatively new on the scene but they have revolutionized the way Americans are preparing for retirement. An FIA allows your money to move out of the stock market, but when the market goes up you'll still go up. You won't go up as much, but you'll still go up significantly more than a CD. When the market goes down, you are protected from market loss because you have a floor. This is the fastest-growing retirement vehicle in the nation.

In 1987, Suze Orman wrote the book, *You've Earned It, Don't Lose It,* after seeing $50,000 that she was given to start a bakery disappear because she followed bad financial advice. She learned all she could about finances and later became a talk show host and a tell-it-like-it-is financial expert, recognized nationwide for her acerbic tongue and her no-nonsense approach to money. She said about FIAs: "If you're willing to give up some upside potential, you can also protect yourself totally from downside risk."

There are no fees associated with FIAs. The principal is guaranteed. Earnings are based on market performance. You benefit from an up market but are protected from losses. Think of a ratchet. When the index upon which your annuity returns are based goes up, you go up with it. You don't get all of the gains. Let's say the market soars 20% one year. Depending on which company you purchased your FIA from, your gain may be 7% or thereabouts. That gain locks in. Then, if the market tumbles 20%, you don't participate in that loss (principal + gains are never lost). That year, zero was your hero. You made zero and you lost zero. You are just waiting for the next market swing so you can ride the crest of that wave to an even higher pinnacle. Over time, the average return on these products is approximately 5-6%. That's not a get-rich-quick rate of return, but not having sleepless nights is a big plus.

Remember the Einstein quote about insanity means doing the same thing over and over again and expecting a different result? I'm sure he was perhaps thinking of solving a math equation, but the principle applies to whose advice we follow when making decisions about our finances. You don't have to be a food chef to understand the difference between an apple and a taco, and you don't have to be a genius to know when something just doesn't make sense.

Comparing Apples to Tacos

CONCLUSION

If you read this book in its entirety, you know retirement planning is not about stock picking, market timing, watching CNN, reading Money Magazine, or blindly following someone who calls himself or herself an advisor. It's about figuring out how you want to live in your retirement and finding a fiduciary who can (and will) help you achieve your goals. You need to find someone who will teach you and help you to learn the rules of retirement and develop a strategy that will enable you to win.

There are a lot of financial planners who call themselves *retirement* planners, but they are merely doing financial planning for older people. Don't listen to the noise, and don't believe the lies. Develop good habits and behaviors that will carry you all the way through the rest of your life. You *can* have a relaxed stress-free, successful retirement. I know, because I help people achieve it every day.

ABOUT THE AUTHOR

Ron Tetley and his wife of 22 years, Teresa, live in Wadsworth, Ohio. They are parents to four children, one married, one in college and two in high school.

Since 1994, Ron has been advising businesses and individuals about financial matters. Ron is a financial coach and president of Creative Retirement Planning, LLC, in Akron, Ohio, a company he co-founded in 2005. His training and experience allow him to offer a full range of services to pre-retirees and retirees. These services include, but are not limited to, investment management, retirement planning, asset protection, distribution, estate planning, income planning, and tax planning.

Ron is also a well-known and nationally recognized financial educator. His candid views and insightful comments have appeared in magazine articles, newspapers, and other forms of the media, as well as in the books and monthly newsletters that he writes.

Ron's expertise is highly sought after by others in the financial industry. He has trained many individuals, as well as marketing organizations, with his no-nonsense approach to investing and retirement planning.